DevOps

The ultimate beginners guide to learn DevOps step-by-step

Mark Reed

Table of Contents

Introduction

It is evident that technology has changed the society at large. Today we live, work, and communicate in ways that seemed incomprehensible only a decade ago. For instance, consider the influence cloud technology has had on information technology. While all the changes resulting from technological advancement are good for business, the new digital technologies also present different challenges for IT and their users. For instance, the high demand for real-time communications and instant software updates have triggered core changes in the IT operations paradigm. Due to such changes, companies are under pressure to get their applications up and running within the shortest time possible.

Notably, IT has facilitated the need to adopt quicker and more agile software management frameworks. As a result, IT life cycles have shortened as applications become more complex. This has in turn facilitated the need for cross-collaboration and integration between different IT constituents such as development, operations, and quality assurance. The result: a new IT discipline referred to as DevOps.

So, the obvious questions to ask at this point are What is DevOps? Does your organization leverage DevOps today? What measures have you put in place to ensure efficient workflows, increased revenue generation, and faster production cycles in your business or company? This book seeks to answer these questions and more, as well as any other questions that beginners have about DevOps. By the time you are done reading this book, you will understand what DevOps is, why your organization needs it, its different applications, and its importance in the modern IT-driven business environment.

DevOps facilitates effective communication and collaboration across an organization. This allows businesses to produce and improve products at a faster rate than they would have if using traditional approaches. Collaboration builds stronger, more productive, and happier teams that are solely focused on end product quality and performance. Operations become seamless, since every individual works towards a common goal. High efficiency not only accelerates development but also streamlines the entire process, making it less prone to costly and time consuming errors. DevOps tasks can be automated, leaving software engineers with more time to focus on executing other, non-automated tasks. This, partly, facilitates the agile relationship between operations departments and system development departments as created by DevOps. Such collaborations offer technically effective results that favor both users and customers.

The industry has set the bar and is implementing DevOps at a high rate. Conversely, organizations are eager to take advantage of the enhanced innovation, stable operations environment, faster application delivery, and building performance-oriented work teams with the aim of maximizing profits. Therefore, it is paramount to understand the essential factors about DevOps and its application in the current business environment. Despite how different people are, all the differences must be set aside when it comes to company management and operations. People must work as one unit in order to achieve the core company goals which are excellent customer service and offering solutions to industry specific problems. If everyone can imbibe this organizational work culture philosophy and take time to understand DevOps, it will be easier to create invaluable workplace practices that value people over profits and processes. Indulge to learn DevOps essentials that you should know!

Chapter One: What Is DevOps?

In simple terms, DevOps refers to a set of practices configured to combine information technology operations with software development to shorten the system development life cycle needed to achieve high-quality software. The word DevOps is derived from "development and operation," which is used to describe the agile relationship that exists between IT operations and software development with an aim to develop better communication in the two fields.

How Was DevOps Derived?

DevOps was initially derived from agile software development in an attempt to keep up with the increased software velocity achieved through the use of agile methods. Moreover, the advancement of the agile culture comprising other prevailing methods over the years has given rise to more holistic approaches to software development that focus on an end-to-end software delivery cycle. Agile software development is essentially a hypernym, and it is used to describe the group of software production strategies built around this systemic approach. It is a methodology that combines two software improvement methods in the industry, one incremental

7

and the other, iterative, into a single system to more efficiently and effectively produce and roll out technological products. These agile methodologies include extreme programming (XP), Lean Development, Kanban, scrum, and scaled agile.

There are many unique agile methodologies, and while there are specific approaches and scenarios suited for each particular method, the different methods all still share the same primary implementation and core values, which derive the similarity between them. They all incorporate an iterative-centered style embedded with a form of a feedback channel for the evolution of projects and software. The methods that consist of feedback channels specifically are considered as the subparts of the main software project. These subparts are responsible for continuous testing, planning, and integration throughout both the software development and deployment process to ensure the unceasing evolution of the software. Moreover, they are regarded as lightweight when compared to the initial and more traditional waterfall-style processes, which are inherently adaptable for reinvention. What is good about agile methods is the fact that it has a primary impact on empowering the people towards making an informed decision effectively.

Initially, agile teams were made up of aggressive and innovative developers, which make these methods popular because of their efficiency and effectiveness when handling the in-depth nature of software development. The aggressiveness and innovation put in place by the agile team ensured that the desired goal was achieved by the organization in question. They create a competitive advantage in the market through unique service delivery, which cannot be easily emulated by other experts. Though the agile team works along with the quality assurance team, these people in particular are responsible for the organization's product output, which makes their service more distinct than others. Instead, they outgrow the quality assurance team in order to deliver an increased velocity software, which ensures that the idea is brought into reality by the experts. Furthermore, the DevOps team focuses on the standardization of the services, which creates an automated environment to improve the software service delivery to potential customers and users in general. It is all about the efficiency, security, and sustainability of the software to ensure that there are no hiccups in the system.

DevOps Roots and Origin

Before delving much on the roots and origin, we have to consider the main intention behind DevOps development. Because it is a set of practices that involves the automation of processes between software developers and IT teams in order to build, test, and release software faster and more effectively and reliably mark it all. Also, its combination of cultural philosophies, practices, skills, and tools that increase the organization's ability to deliver software application and of a higher quality play a vital role in its development.

It is the term for a group of concepts that, while not all new, have triggered into a movement and are increasingly spreading throughout the technical community. The new concept arises from the collision of two major related trends in which the first was called "agile infrastructure" or "agile operations." The second is a much-expanded understanding of operations staff throughout all stages of information technology and software development.

Moreover, DevOps automation can be derived by repackaging platforms, systems, and applications into reusable building blocks through the use of technologies. These comprise virtual machines and containerization DevOps systems majorly based on division of labor. Each team member focuses and relies on different criteria to evaluate their efficiency in an organizational setup to enhance the delivery of highly developed software products and good quality. It is the practice of operations and development engineers participating together in the entire service life cycle, from design through the development process to production support.

As technologies were evolving and business needs were becoming more dynamic and sophisticated, it was evident that the existing approach to implementing projects had to be adjusted. As a result, the agile manifesto was born, allowing for more productive teamwork between developers and quality assurance engineers on top of other important things like the ability to change requirements on the go and launch projects much faster and easier. The essence of Agile development narrows down to a series of short cycles called "iterations," which usually take about two or three weeks or even a month. In its turn, each iteration is considered as a mini or a micro project and includes such steps as requirements analysis, planning, implementation, testing, and documenting.

Comparably, Google was not the only company to start employing SREs and soon enough, all the big tech players began to implement site reliability philosophies to reduce downtime and increase customer satisfaction to enable them to achieve great profits. In 2008, Apple experienced significant downtime in which the nascent cloud service received a lot more traffic to servers than anticipated. Due to proving downtime or angry customers, they began to experience huge losses that could otherwise deteriorate the company's image and financial position.

Through their experience managing uptime at the world's largest photo-sharing site at the time, Allspaw and Hammond noted that the operations team, charged with managing servers, and the development team, the team tasked with creating code, seemed to always be at odds with each other and more often than not, were "finger-pointing" instead of solving problems. The blame game had become too much, and they had realized that this was going to cause much harm to the organization. They, therefore, needed to come up with strategies to manage this condition and help them solve the problem at hand.

The solution they proposed was to hire operation employees who think like developers and engineers and developers who think like operators. In a presentation at the 2009 O'Reilly Velocity conference, Allspaw and Hammond proposed integrating development and operations into a singular automated infrastructure with shared version control and one-step build and deployment. John Allspaw and Paul Hammond were Flickr engineers, and through them, DevOps was born, but it did not have a name yet. The main aim of starting DevOps was to ensure faster delivery of software products in a developing tech world and to enhance a culture of teamwork. This culture developed with time, and other firms were quick in adopting it because it was convenient and reliable.

Factually, DevOps is here to stay for the foreseeable future until some new methodology or technology comes along to replace it and disrupt its space. It is the offspring of agile software development born from the need to keep up with the increased software velocity through agile methodologies. We are already witnessing signs of DevOps maturing and evolving into something more advanced and trendy.

Artificial intelligence is starting to permeate everything from smartphones to self-driving cars that have been developed into the first moving technological world. It will also help disrupt the DevOps mantra to automate better. This DevOps culture is even making it easier for scholars to improve their technological abilities, thereby improving their technological skills. Besides, it is leaning towards the concept of thinking combined and blended with agile philosophy. The revolutionary DevOps perception of DevOps is that it crosses a traditional line by merging software development with the environment in which it was founded and developed. This cultural change is then made possible by several tools that automate such processes as code development and review through continuous integration while making it possible by merging different functions and roles from software testing to the deployment of the software, which makes it complete.

Rationally, the rise of DevOps is not all that new to the current generation of youths. Information Technology has a history of ensuring relevance to more and more people all the time. What was once walled off in its department with corporations and learning institutions has now spread all over the world and into everyone's pocket. DevOps takes the next logical step in this growth and development by bringing together or at least linking, development, and operations to create a schedule of activity in which everyone can participate.

Furthermore, it was the inevitable outcome of building and operating sites that became the web giants. In the 21st century, developers cannot just create new features in the lab and then expect operations to take over and deploy the current software. They need to understand how these systems work and how they are configured and deployed because it is installed across thousands of machines, both virtual and physical. However, they need to collaborate with the Ops team to build and maintain the deployment process because that deployment is now software.

The main problem with the DevOps team is a risk of security issues because the security team is not integrated with DevOps, and they have no idea about tactics and methodologies being used to speed up the application development process. Therefore, adapting the DevOps system will require major change and adaptation in the mindset of employees and employers and organizational culture as a whole, which cannot happen overnight because it will take quite some time.

Why Is DevOps Required?

Since DevOps tend to describe a culture and a set of resources which mainly focused on the development and operation advancement of the software, it ensures that the organizations can create and improve a product faster. When compared to traditional software, it is somehow advanced and adored by many people who embrace the new technology. The fact that DevOps has a shorter development cycle makes it very unique and necessary in the new technological advancement in society. Though the development and operation teams may exist in different silos, one cannot easily tell when the application is likely to be ready for use. However, when the application has been turned over by the developers, it tends to gain faster acceptance and readily used within the shortest time possible. These initiatives tend to extend the operation cycle of development of the new technological advancement, which attracts the major population in the market today.

Naturally, the company needs to develop the application within the shortest time possible, thus making it attractive and economical in terms of production cost and the overhead expenditure incurred during the invention. In fact, it is estimated by Red Hat official, Kevin Murphy that the shorter development period translates to a faster market percentage, which ensures that there are a great growth and market penetration within the shortest period possible.

Moreover, DevOps development is important in such a way that it reduces deployment failure, which is likely to happen with any other company. Also, time to recover and rollbacks are looked into by the company, which ensures that there is a great allocation for resources that do not inconvenience the development of the application. It has been identified that most of the programming failure leads to deployment failure, which is not common with the DevOps. With shorter development cycles, the company enjoys frequent code release, which ensures that any defect which may inconvenience the development is spotted before its full manifestation. Therefore, there is a reduced number of deployment failure which may occur in the system, thus ensuring that there is a continuer's involvement of the employees throughout the development phase. By employing the agile programming principles which aid in collaboration and modular programming in the corporation, rollbacks easily managed since it can only occur when the module is affected which has a minimal chance to happen.

Moreover, time to recover is an important issue in system development since some failures have to anticipate. It is important to have a time recovery in which a platform for interaction provided by both parties working on the system development. They get humble time to share and develop the ideas, which may turn out to be very crucial in the development of the system, thus eliminating the challenges which may exist. Gathering the ideas from a different perspective or diverse view makes the decision-making process easier and fruitful for all those who are involved. It is not a matter of credit to be earned but the desire to have a great outcome. They are being driven by the desire to achieve great technological advancement, which aims at changing lives of millions. It is humanity at its best and not self-desire to get rich or get the recognition from the general public.

Additionally, DevOps are required because they improve communication and collaboration in software development culture. The culture of development primarily focuses on the performance of the entity rather than the individual goals, which are common among other companies. In this concept, teams trust each other, and they carry out their experiments and innovation effectively to deliver quality software. From this perspective, the teams may decide to focus on getting the product to market in the shortest time possible or either focus on the production whereby the KPIs of the entity is structured accordingly towards achieving the desired goal.

In this case, the production and turn out of events has nothing to do with the "turning over" of the application, which may await what will happen in the future. It depends on the current situation of the system update or development created by the expert team. The operation does not have to wait for other team members to troubleshoot the problem to fix it desirably. Since all the team individuals work towards achieving the same goal projected by the organization, the process increasingly becomes seamless.

Furthermore, with increased efficiency, there is an elevation in the development process with devoid of errors during the advancement period of the software. Most of the tasks of DevOps are automated with continuous integration servers, which aid in testing the codes to automate the system for effectiveness and efficiency. By doing so, there is a decreased annual work required by the system. On the other hand, software engineers do focus on completing the tasks which cannot be automated by the system.

The system developers have accelerating tools that aid in increasing the efficiency of the system. These tools include scalable infrastructure, which is integrated into the system in the form of cloud-based platforms which aid the access to hardware resource by the team. As a result of this, there are chances that the testing and deployment rate of operation speed up in the process. Moreover, there are build acceleration tools that aid at compiling code very fast in the system, thus increasing the efficiency of the software operation. Furthermore, with a parallel workflow embedded in the system, there is continues chain delivery whereby the teams have not to wait for others to deliver is when to commence with work at hand. Besides, there is a shared environment where the team members do not have to transfer data between different environments, which may incur some faulty practices. One does not need to use the same environment for the whole development of the system. Therefore, there is a need to test different environments and the other for deployment purposes of software development.

Ultimately, the DevOps comes with reduced costs and IT headcount, which is necessary for the development. According to software management, Red Hat Corporation needs 35% less IT staff to work in a DevOps-oriented system, which lowers the cost of operations. The fact remains that every company needs people to work for the same company, but the chances are low that they get the desired job there. The only outstanding factor is the quality of their work, which makes them distinct from the rest and the way they can maximize the output through their input. From the industrial perspective, implementing DevOps at a rapid rate ensures that there is faster application delivery to potential customers at a convenient time. By doing so, there are a stable operation, innovativeness, and performance-focused employees who have the same aim of providing convenient operation software. It is believed that when one uses the open-source DevOps tools, they can easily power up their proprietary IT vendors within themselves within no time. Besides, the DevOps technologies provide consulting services which ensure that the client has a freedom of choice and the flexibility to integrate the system whenever they need it in their home devices.

Who Is a DevOps Engineer?

The person who understands the software development cycle and writes the software code is considered to be the DevOps engineer responsible for the system. There are more responsibilities assumed by these people who are behind the breakthrough of this technological advancement. Though there is more involved in the process to make the whole thing successful where others can vouch for it, remember that technological advancement happens every day, and one cannot stick to the same knowledge overtime. Room for adjustment is provided, which enables the inventor to encounter problems which may recur appropriately without much hiccups on the development.

As explained above, DevOps is a software strategically developed to bridge the gap between the IT staff and developers, which ensures efficiency in technology development. The world is evolving, and we cannot stick at one specific technological standpoint where we were a century ago. By following such a notion of evolution, we have to catch up with the latest technology lest we are left behind. Besides, the tech companies have been able to experience fewer or fewer software failures over the past few years' credits to DevOps, which makes the difference in the market today. The engineers involved have been able to overcome the traditional limitation of the former worn-out models, which are not effective anymore in the new technological error. There has been much development, deployment of technologies, testing for the automated CI involved in the process to make it effective and efficient for use.

Moreover, there are some of the famous tools of DevOps, which make it easier for engineers to carry out their duties effectively. These tools include Git and Github, which are the source of code management for the system. It ensures that the codes do not leak to the outside intruder, which can intrude the system thus making it vulnerable. Also, the engineers are responsible for creating Jenkins which are the automation servers. These servers are used as plugins built in such a way that they develop a CD pipeline. Apart from the mentioned tools, there are puppets, chefs, and ansible use for configuration management and deployment of the software and these are supported by Nagios, which are used for monitoring the system operation.

By now, one should be able to understand the tools which are used by the DevOps engineer before analyzing their responsibilities. Nevertheless, before that, one should know that these people are the main brains behind the development of the software, where they link up with the IT experts to make it successful. They can also assume the responsibility of the main developers without the assistance of the IT team, where they take responsibility for network operation and deployment, which is made easier by the passion of scripting and coding. By doing so, engineers can focus on the development and planning test.

Classically, there are various roles played by the DevOps developers, which make it a success at the end of the day. Foremost, there is a DevOps evangelist who is primarily responsible for implementing the software. The evangelist is supported by the release manager, who is responsible for the new feature release whereby the person ensures that the product is stable before its release to the market. From this point, there is an automation expert who is responsible for the orchestration and automation of the tools to make the software stable and desirable for use by everyone. After which there is a software tester or developer responsible for code creation and test before it is incorporated into the system for use. The chain is not complete until it passes through the quality assurance team who must ensure that it meets the quality required and confirm it that it is good for us. From this point, it will be released to the market, but the security engineers will still monitor its health and security throughout to ensure that everything is okay.

What Is the Job Description for the DevOps Engineer?

That is a common question in any technical field since it attracts much interest from many people. Most of the students aspire to be DevOps engineers, and for them to achieve their dreams, they need to know what it takes to be an engineer and what to expect apart from the qualifications they can acquire. Therefore, this brings us to the fundamental aspect of an engineer, and we tend to look at the qualifications need for the work at hand, what they need to offer for the service they are seeking, and the time taken to accomplish such tasks. It is not a surprise that some people get into some jobs with an expectation that things will eventually change in the future, not knowing that some tend to remain constant for a long time. For engineering jobs like a DevOps developer, one needs to possess some skills which will enable them to be effective and efficient in what they do,how they do it and the process it takes. Initially, one needs to acquire one cloud platform knowledge, and it can come in form of Azure, GCP or AWS. These must be regarded as the most important aspects of being a qualified engineer in this field.

Moreover, for one to be safe, one needs to get good knowledge in configuration management and be conversant with the deployment tools such as Chef, Puppet, Terraform, and Ansible. This knowledge cannot stand on their own without being proficient in scripting and Git workflows in a proper manner. Besides, there is a need to have great experience in developing continuous integration.

The salary of a DevOps engineer is also important to take into consideration. In this case, one should examine the salary of the service to see if it is worth the hustle. The funny fact that not all companies pay engineers the same salary, but it depends on other prevailing factors involved in the process. Company A will always pay differently with company B, and in most cases, the company paying highest also retrenches other employees to create space. Back to the main point, the salary has much to do with the agreement between the employer and the employee. Most of the DevOps engineers are paid an average of $121,589 per year.

The approximation has been reached through examining about 18,434 of employees from the past and present employees of different organizations. However, it depends on the country of operation where one is employed. So do not expect to be paid the same depending on the country one works at in any given day. For that reason, there is a need to carry out due diligence when searching for a job. Though some people are lucky in the job market and they are prone to get first-class jobs with little or no hustle. In that case, those who are not into the market yet will inquire from different agencies which tend to give different contract term. It is all about developing skills as one continues with the work or train at work as they progress.

Chapter Two:
The DevOps Lifecycle and Workflow

Many people from the software industry might have a bit of an idea of what DevOps is all about. Nevertheless, to understand the concept, there is a need to know the DevOps lifecycle and failure to do so renders one illiterate of the entire concept. My main concern in this chapter is to give insight on what the DevOps lifecycle is and how it works to make technological advancement complete. Moreover, the need to help my reader understand DevOps in all perspectives is greater than anything else, and if one can grasp this concept in its entirety, then one is good to go!

It is prudent to remember that before the existence of DevOps, there were other technological advancements in the market that were not as efficient as DevOps, thus making the DevOps more essential. There was other software like the waterfall model incorporated with a related agile model for software development. One should understand the former models and how they work before moving on to the new model we have at hand. Just like any other modern technological advancement, the model's history and origin is extremely more important to make the current situation worth the coin. How can one know or understand their current status or achieve their current economic state without knowledge of how the past played into their life? I am not making this personal but am trying to make it more understandable and clear to anyone who intends to grasp the full concept of the matter. By doing so, we can move forward in uniformity without any glitch or worry.

Therefore, we have to review the waterfall model and how it works before commencing with the DevOps concept. In this case, the waterfall model is considered the sequential process in software development, which entails a top-down approach. The model is considered to be a linear and straight-forward model in the making. In this concept, there were various phases involved in its development to make it viable and complete. The phases of its development include defining requirements, designing, and implementing processes, then software testing and deployment, and finally software maintenance once released.

The software companies that used this kind of model approach spent much of their time researching, assembling the requirements, and making the project complete. The team had to complete the first phase before proceeding to the next phase, thus demanding, in each phase, much involvement to make everything right before getting to the next level. Such thinking encompassed the whole process unlike in DevOps development, in which the whole phase can be done by different teams at the same time without any complications involved. Also, in the waterfall approach, the final phase was determined by the working software, which had to be completed after considering all the processes involved.

One should ascertain that the waterfall model was only suitable for projects which had a concrete requirement in place. What do I mean by concrete requirements? It basically insinuates that the requirement of software development does not change over time. From this perspective, one can notice that there is nothing static in the tech world; things change from day to day, making software development more advanced and complex. The traditional waterfall model insinuates that everything had to remain the same for software to exist, manifest, and become effective. We cannot live with the same notion, nor shall we believe that there will be no change in the future concerning technological advancements. Imagine a situation in which one has to live the same kind of life every day. Doing the same thing that they did yesterday, today, and in the future. Therefore, there were drawbacks associated with the waterfall model that rendered it obsolete. Some of these drawbacks include the project timeline, static requirements, and intense involvement demanded by the model.

The agile methodology practice promotes a continuous iteration that incorporates testing throughout the software's development lifecycle. It is worth noting that both testing and development activities in this methodology are concurrent, unlike in the waterfall model, in which they were static. This methodology focuses more on agility to development and as a result, it may be lost during operations that do not materialize into viable practices. Moreover, there was no collaboration between the developers and engineers responsible for its operation rendering ineffective.

After understanding all it took in the past to come up with software, let us go back to our initial objective.

What Is the Lifecycle of DevOps?

DevOps focuses on the relationship between the operation and the development of the software. Here, the engineers and developers have the same objective to deliver a viable product with the same goal in mind: to make the product perfect and suitable for use for all inhabitants. Therefore, for one to understand the whole concept, there is a need to capture the DevOps lifecycle to make the project complete. The complete life cycle of this methodology has seven phases, which must be considered before arriving at the complete package of the software.

These include continuous:

- Development
- Integration
- Testing
- Monitoring
- Feedback
- Deployment
- Operation

With the right implementation of the life cycle of DevOps, one can achieve much and make apps more secure and effective for use. DevOps entails the latest technology and the need to make it summarize the whole concept into reality. It is worth saying that the DevOps concept is dependable and worth the investment since it proves to be more efficient and effective to the largest global enterprises.

Those who are still skeptical or still wonder if DevOps is a reality or another far-fetched tale about Silicon Valley are behind reality themselves. Based on the rapid development and demand in the technology market, nothing is worth the investment more than the DevOps software. Though, there is swift demand in the IT sector where there is a need to update systems daily, depending on the market demand. Due to that, the need to create new versions is inevitable. All are bound to continuity in the system development.

1. Continuous development

Continuous development is the initial stage of the DevOps lifecycle. Here, the application objectives are aligned to the goals to be achieved by the developers to meet the customer's demand. At this stage, the application objectives and code requirements are taken into consideration and set by the developers. Once the developers have set the objectives of the project, they can start project development without delay. Code generators and other needed software are initiated and developed at this phase, and these projects have to follow the continuous development approach initiated by the developers to make the viable and suitable in the preceding stages. The existing code is used for continuous feedback in the development of the whole scheme operation.

One should remember that there are no DevOps tools required when making the plan; the code will require several tools for its maintenance, however. Moreover, code can be written in any language as long as they are relevant to the project at hand, where it is maintained using the version control tools. Source code management is the term used by the IT experts for maintaining the codes in the system. In this case, there are various popular tools used by the developers for managing the codes like Mercurial, SVN, JIRA, and CVS used by the experts. When it comes to continuous development, there is an intense use of

Maven, Ant, and Gradle tools. Most developers prefer Gradle for packaging the code into a feasible and executable file, which can be moved to the next phase easily.

Git is a version control tool used in supporting non-linear workflows in the system where it provides data assurance. One has to employ this tool to guarantee quality software suitable for the project. Besides, it ensures that there is a proper communication channel between the developers and the operation team in the project being carried out by the company. It is important to have a clear communication channel where a large project is concerned to make it easier for collaborators to make changes in time, thus modifying the system to suit the situation. Git plays a crucial role in communication among the team, whereby it creates a stable version of the project application where the team can interact and reach a conclusion based on the prevailing factors at hand. Hence, for DevOps to succeed, Git must be incorporated in the system to ensure proper communication channels.

2. Continuous integration

The process of continuous integration automatically starts after the development stage. It can also be shortened as CI in DevOps in the build pipeline or lifecycle. As we all know, there is a single control tool for both the operation and development team where all the codes are derived for a common purpose. Codes are consolidated into a master code, on which everyone has the liberty to work by themselves.

Under continuous integration, there are other processes involved which make it concrete to its cause. After merging the developer's codes, the DevOps team is responsible for triggering a build in the system where the codes are compiled to arrive at the concrete software code to be used. It then undergoes a unit test to verify its responsiveness to the project developed. Moreover, there is a server for the control tools used by the system developers during continuous integration where the code check-in is looked into, and as soon as any triggers are found, an automation compilation is issued for security checking. Here, automated testing is carried out by tools such as TestNG, Jenkins, and NUnit for static solar analysis. The fundamental objective behind carrying out continuous integration is to ensure that the developer's code run smoothly, and any error detected is corrected in time to avoid inconveniences. The developer can detect and know if they are in the right channel of coding or not by the aid of these control tools.

It will compare the codes of all the developers within the organization and ensure that the codes are within the correct line of action. In a nutshell, we can say that the CI is concerned with the integrity of the code, whether they are within acceptable terms for the project and the basis for its plan test before building the product. It checks if the team members can produce the right code for system integration. After these processes have been verified, the team is in a position to proceed to the next phase of development.

3. Continuous testing

At this stage, products are verified by the responsible team for their actual usage in a normal environment. The testing process essentially tests how the application will be used and if it meets quality assurance specifications. The testing process gives much information about the different application aspects and how they are integrated into the system before it is sent to the development process. The developers test for bugs in the system to ensure that it is effective and updated with the latest version. In this case, automation testing tools like TestNG, Selenium, and Junit are used. These tools ensure that there are no flaws in the functionality, and that the quality of the code is on point. Though there are chances of non-functionality in the system, these should not be accepted by the developers, thus the need to pass code through the testing process to eliminate such errors.

The testing tools, such as Selenium, are used to automate the system in such a way that it generates reports. The whole testing phase is modified by the developers so that other tools are automated in the system to ensure that no error penetrates during the development of the DevOps lifecycle. If a person has written a Selenium code in Java, one can advance this using Ant or Maven to improve the application code initially used by the developer to build the code. In this case, the automation of the codes ensures that time is saved, and the codes are used effectively towards achieving the set objective of the system. Instead of integrating the codes manually, one ought to automate the codes to fulfill the need for coding and application requirements. Also, the codes can be integrated with the existing codes to make it perfect and desirable for the system to execute the processes needed by the developers. It makes things easier for developers and the operation team when there are existing codes to be modified to fit the needs of the software. Imagine taking a leap of faith to start the whole process again when the project is under a strict timeline, which cannot be achieved without deep knowledge of what is needed. It tends to be hard, but with existing codes, few modifications are required to make it stand out on its own.

This stage is crucial for DevOps development since it entails almost all that is needed to be done during the software's development. The source code must be changed frequently in the system for it to succeed. However, this may be done every week or daily, depending on the prevailing need at the market.

Every commit is built on the system to detect any error which may arise from the codes developed by the programmers for the software. Besides, there is a code review, and not only compilation is done at this level of development. There is also unit testing, packaging, and integration testing, which may be carried out by developers to ensure that the software becomes stable and sustainable for a long time without any problems. All that matters to people is the dependability and efficacy of the system, not how it was coded or integrated to work. The final product is the determinant of the whole system's sustainability and profitability. What is the need of developing something which cannot stand for itself, or software which lacks flexibility and cannot be modified to fit the current need of the customers? However, with DevOps, the system is verified, tested, and proved to be suitable for the final use.

4. Continuous monitoring

The monitoring phase is an operational process whereby the product information is reviewed for any errors that may arise in the system for sustainability. It involves recording application usage and processing trends on how it functions via a monitoring tool, which ensures that there is little or no error incurred during a coding session. Developer and operation teamwork is reviewed and analyzed to ensure that they are suitable. It is important to monitor the system's stability and development. Apart from monitoring the way it operates, the team looks into various hazards that the system may be subjected to during its operation time. The system errors, which may present themselves as memory or server unavailabilities are resolved at this phase of development.

Here, the vital information of the system is monitored and recorded by the DevOps tools. By doing so, the developer can determine the cause of any error which may occur before it manifests beyond repair. It serves as a warning to any emerging issues that may recur in software sustainability and stability for future demands. The need to foresee the future makes the creator of the code more insightful to avoid any problems with future modifications of the system. One should not create an unmodifiable system that is rendered obsolete as soon as a new model emerges. To the employees, creating an unsustainable product that cannot reach market demands is not cause for confidence. It is worth protecting the reputation of the company and the self-image more so where technology is concerned.

Critically, there are security issues that need to be protected by the developers lest one loses the whole system to fraudulent people who are out there to hawk it whenever they get a chance to do so. It does not matter the worth of the investment, and all that matters is the safety of the system. DevOps use Splunk to monitor the system and protect it from intruders.

5. Continuous feedback

This phase is strategically used to improvise the current product in harmony with the prevailing demand in the market. The developers analyze the existing product to improve its usage to adapt to modern demand. Here the customer feedback about the product is taken into consideration, and any complaint is acted upon within the best timeframe possible to eliminate any sluggishness or compiling complaints. This is the biggest asset of the company and should be protected by all means possible. The current working software is updated frequently to ensure that it does not incur many problems and to meet the customer's needs.

6. Continuous deployment

At this stage, the developers and operation team work together to ensure that the product released has no error. The product is reviewed for maximum accuracy to ensure that changes made in the code do not affect the efficiency of the system, thus ensuring that high traffic to the website is achieved.

7. Continuous operations

The last phase of the DevOps lifecycle, software is released to the market to execute its duties. It is based on complete automation of the released process to accelerate the overall time to market. Continuity is the critical factor in DevOps. Though it may take more time to identify issues, it is the best version for system modification.

Chapter Three:
DevOps Practices

Integration

DevOps critically relies on software engineering, which brings about practices that ensure improved efficiency of the organization software system. However, there are considerations to be made when integrating DevOps systems, such as team choice. In most cases, the team chosen to carry out the task does not fit the specifications needed by the organization, thus leading to failure or shoddy service delivery. This kind of development has to be looked into lest the organization is doomed to failure. Therefore, to subdue that, an integrated change management should be put in place to oversee the basic requirements and team workflow in the organization. Change management members are tasked with ensuring that there is a successful and meaningful evolution of the IT infrastructure that supports the overall organization's well-being and general growth. Though, it may be tricky at the project team level to meet the objectives since there is more technicality involved and one cannot use a single plan to arrive at the solutions and requirements of the project at hand. Also, there is a high probability of DevOps to bring the enterprise issues associated with operations and development of code into the mix, thus creating the need for integrated change management, which is essential at all levels of the software development. Hence, the development teams must work closely with operations team into the mix to enhance the efficiency and effectiveness of the software.

Furthermore, integrated deployment planning is put into action by the developers to create a strategic plan on how to employ different resources to achieve the set objectives of the organization. On the deployment planning, one is required to interact with an organization's operations staff in order to build a sustainable relationship vital for the team performance. Besides, the experienced development teams are obliged to carry out such planning practices continuously throughout construction with active stakeholder participation from different departments like operations, development, and support groups. When someone adopts a DevOps strategy, they quickly realize the need to take a cross-team approach to deployment planning due to the need for operations staff, but it can also be a surprise to development teams accustomed to working in their own environments.

Critically, there is an integrated configuration management team that ensures that the development teams not only apply CM at the solution level, as is customary of the other software companies. DevOps also consider production configuration issues between their solution and the rest of the organization's infrastructure. However, the working environment is regarded as an important asset for the developers. Due to that, they are well acquainted with the responsibility to create enterprise-aware software and focus on the bigger picture in achieving the set objectives. How will their solution work and take other assets in production? The implication is that development teams will need to understand and manage the full range of dependencies for their product to avoid incurring losses and to fully take account of financial transactions daily. Integrated configuration management enables operations staff to understand the potential result of new software release, thus enhancing easy decisions on when to allow the new software release to occur.

One should also consider the continuous integration process as the greatest tool in ensuring that the software is stable and able to carry out the intended functions. In short, it is the art of creating and validating a project before releasing it to the market. It employs an automated regression testing and, at times, includes the use of code analysis software tool. Whenever an updated code is checked into the version control system, it detects any error that may exist and makes the correction immediately. To ease the process, CI is incorporated as one of the sexier agile development practices from a developer's understanding, which is typically associated with DevOps stability.

Delivery

After learning about continuous integration in DevOps software, one can now understand the full concept of how continuous delivery is developed to fulfill the intended purpose of technological advancement. Moreover, it can be stated as an important process of the software update to ensure an increment in software released to the market. Within the corporation and within different department teams, the software is made ready for delivery at any given point as long as the required specification had been made.

So, what is term delivery? Typically, it is a life cycle of code in which new code is developed by the team and tested at different stages. The testing can be done manually or through automated stage gates, and it ensures that the end product is conducive and desired by the organization. From this perspective, the main aim of continuous delivery is to meet the customer's demand and make things right as soon as possible, thus ensuring a short development cycle.

Therefore, there are some of the benefits of continuous delivery, which make it worth the full venture in DevOps development. First, it increases the frequency of delivery to potential clients. Here, clients can access the product more frequently and still find it worth their coin. On the other hand, the organization can make a profit out of the delivery service, thus making it a profitable and stable business. Nevertheless, all these cannot be done without proper planning, which ensures that there is minimal production failure at the enterprise. Also, the frequent delivery process ensures that there is reduced manual work within the company and all the employees are economically engaged in such a way that they complete the circuit well. All that matters to employees is the good reputation of the organization, and when developers' concerns are regarded as important, it increases their confidence as a team, thus creating chances of high productivity. By doing so, the team can automate the system in such a way that it caters to the organizational needs, ensuring that there is faster feedback of the system.

Factually, the delivery is all about the increment in value to customers, which ensures that the demand is met within the time limit. The team should always be ready to deliver any time of the day whenever called upon to do so at a given set timeline. For them to fulfill that, they must commit to working specifications. Thus, the continuous delivery primarily concerns the life cycle of code in which the code is initially developed, tested, or updated at different stages. The process can be done manually or automated depending on the needs of the organization, and then it passes through other automated stage gates before it reaches the full production level.

So, the greatest intention of continuous delivery is to create value for the customer's money, whereby the clients can receive services more frequently at the lowest cost possible. DevOps is highly efficient, and there are few irregularities involved in the process, making it more effective and true to its cause. Hence, the product can be marketed at a lower price than traditionally-minded competitors. Moreover, the organization does not deliver filler or junk code to clients, and the products are highly reliable and flexible to customers' needs at the time they need them without much ado between the process.

Typically, CD embraces full system automation, making the cycle complete and reliable whereby the development team begins with code check-in; they then compile and build the code, after which programmers run unit test automation and later complete the circuit with acceptance testing. These are all done until the code in a production pipeline is fully automated and can be deployed by the pipeline. In this case, the DevOps emphasis on continuous delivery can also be referred to as automated deployment pipeline. It involves manual testing that is integrated to be user-friendly, thus enabling it to run to the end user in an acceptable manner, making it easy to use.

How else can one get such user-friendly software if not from DevOps developers and operators? The clients get the value of their money where it conveniences their need at the right place and time. This is achieved through user acceptance testing done by developers to ensure that all is well and following the description.

So, one can perceive all processes and come up with a tangible conclusion on how to benefit from DevOp's invention. Naturally, the continuous delivery process involves two pipelines working hand in hand to make the whole process complete and sustainable. There is one build on the continuous integration, which primarily builds triggers for deploying, compiling, and building software. The other is composed of a pipeline that deals with continuous testing of the process.

Additionally, automating the process reduces the workload, thus making the development faster and more efficient with an increased production rate. These can boost employee morale, since they know that their work does not produce many errors after the chain has been established. In this case, employee mindset focuses on quality and not quantity like in other software companies. All that matters is the reliability, flexibility, and adaptability of the system to the end user. Moreover, what could be the need to have a system that is unreliable, inefficient, and constantly prone to hawker's infringement, which interrupts its functionality? The continuous delivery enriches both operation and development to automate the pipeline to operate effectively. These ensure that the system is functional, secure, and reliable to the end user by efficient automation, which has been highly deployed and tested.

Ultimately, it is worth saying that continuous delivery ensures that the system adopts a short deployment cycle, which enables the team to get feedback within the shortest time possible. With the feedback in place, the developers can easily improve the system towards the customer's specifications. Remember that customers are always right, and whenever in business, their views and concerns matter for the company to be profitable. Nothing is as satisfying as having loyal customers who are always happy with the products, and it makes one feel complete.

Support Practices

Naturally, DevOps advocates for constant collaboration between the IT operation and the development team. The support practice of DevOps revolves around constant communication between these departments to break the culture of collaboration and silos which exist at the organization. However, DevOps practices have been adopted by other software companies to make them realistic and viable over time. Some companies like Netflix, Google, and Amazon have seriously adopted this software developmental method as their own, using it in everything from marketing to back-end development.

Whenever there is a new launch of a new product in the company, it is the responsibility of the IT department to make the product work through proper system integration. Moreover, there is a cultural practice to ensure that the new product is properly marketed by the concerned parties to create awareness in the market. Frustrated customers are aligned in such a way that they accept the new feature created without much involvement. Normally, people fear change, but in technology, change is the competitive advantage created by the incorporation that intends to soar higher in the market. They create an environment suitable for all the parties in the economy. In order to achieve that, the developers must create unique features that mark as the competitive advantage and are environmentally accepted by those involved in the development as well as the customers. Though there exist different methodologies between the IT agents and the developers, these differences should be harmonized to come up with a unique feature that meets the objective of the company. Team involvement ensures that the organization achieves the set goals within the stipulated time as soon as they set on working on it without any complications.

Normally, there is a range of challenges that exist within the organization that can affect the support team, thus limiting them from functioning as required. There are chances that the data required is limited or so scattered that they cannot be harmonized to derive the required code for the software. Such incidences create problems of understanding where the developers and the operation team cannot reach an understanding of what to use for system development. Apart from that, there could also exist deployment failure in the system, which risks the company to its downtime. Most of the time, changes made by the developers and the operation team do not involve the IT team, who tend to complicate the whole process towards their own goals, which does not help the situation. However, there is support feedback that usually represents the customer's views and reaction towards the software features. In such situations, the communication between the customers and the developers plays a large role in ensuring that the product breaks through in the market. It ensures that the product managers create a unique customer care unit that channels all the complaints and views of the customers needed for development towards the company support team.

DevOps are prone to culture change, which determines the collaboration and commitment of the team. This approach ensures that the participants commit towards a common goal and objective. By doing so, there is a shift of mindset created from silos towards working together as a team with the same set of objectives. How else can such be achieved if not by creating a conducive environment with the same cause of action? In this case, it creates a convenient service delivery that encompasses all the software needs in the market. The technology market is expanding every day, and without proper adaptation and flexibility, developers are likely to fail at what they know how to do well. For rapid iteration, companies have been able to collaborate popular approaches like Lean, Agile, and Kanban to facilitate faster information sharing. This is simply through limiting feedback loops, which is responsible for driving business agility.

In the past years, IT had dominated the market by building a strong governance model, which,based on ITIL, is not easy to do away with overnight. While creating new approach to fit the existing technology is not easy, chances are high that they can be imitated and developed into new technology. One of the most influential breakthroughs is CAMA, which was made by John Willis and Edwards at DevOps day in Mountainview back in 2010.

The development of DevOps relies on the cultural practice of the company, which determines its development aspect. There is a cultural shift that ensures the development of the command and control system of the whole software's capability and involvement. Normally, DevOps depends on the speed and agility of the system to make the system flexible and sustainable. With a weekly or daily ritual towards the same objective makes, the cultural shift ensures that there is a daily standup for the development of the software. Moreover, the development and operation team has a chatroom through which they brainstorm how to come up with appropriate code for the software. From this perspective, the organization team can come up with appropriate strategy to fill the gap created in the system.

Furthermore, one needs to focus on the actual result to achieve the purpose of the developers. Anything without focus cannot be actualized by the changes made by the programmers and developers, which makes it viable and attainable to meet the market demand. On the other hand, automation is taking over system sustainability to make things move faster, whereby the process is in support of the development. Here, errors are tracked, and after detection, they are rendered useless thorough diagnosis of the system. This is done regularly to keep the system healthy, whereby it can adopt any change easily whenever there is a need to do so. In addition, articles and other problem-solving strategies are incorporated to ensure that there is an easy way of actualizing the improvement tasks. The teams are made responsible for the documentation and ticket linking to make it efficient and effective for the intended purpose.

Architecture and Risk Mitigation

Architecture-related activities of DevOps are explicitly entailed by a disciplined agile (DA) toolkit, which contains the role of the owner architecture. The whole package primarily used to promote the philosophy of the enterprise to help create awareness. From the company's experience, the architecture work of the project proves to be the core mindset behind the whole process carried out by the organization to achieve the required output. It ensures that the company is at per with the required development. On top of this, there are strategies put in place to ensure that DevOps activities are put in place as the original plan.

Promoting the reuse mindset by the IT architecture ensures that important activities are captured in the system during development. With the reuse mindset, the team can leverage existing data usage through various concepts and frameworks, which ensure that it works well. In order to create the mindset reuse, one has to adopt different training mentality, which may include coaching, educational seminars, or mentoring the architect's activities, which ensures that the IT delivery teams are updated and roles to be played are a good outline for their functionality. Moreover, it ensures that the roadmap of service delivery is up to date and as per the requirement. Besides, it creates a roadmap that is similar to the IT delivery system to capture the high-quality assets to discover and understand the needed real value of the stakeholders.

Similarly, one can adopt the technical-debt mindset, which ensures that the architecture personnel creates the strategies towards getting the pay down debts. The team is motivated to avoid the things which do not necessarily meet the specifications of the requirement. However, without the technical mindset put in place, the delivery team are within the specifications designed by the technical team. In most instances, the acting architecture owners create a tutorial system through which the developers can have the best sub-way forward on how to get full collaborative technical debt. The technical mindset also ensures that the investment in the system does not involve technical debts, which may not inconvenience the IT team. In this case, the technical team is in the hand of the investment team who determine the general appearance of the project.

Furthermore, there is an important aspect of the enterprise, which involves the development guidelines for the whole project. The organization may develop a security guideline necessary for the connectivity of the whole coding standard and another form of special technicality. It is perceived that that architecture layout, which follows the right procedures under strict guidelines tends to produce a persistence outcome that enables them to produce the right outcome. Nevertheless, in case there is any drawback in the process, developers tend to catch up with the constraint which follows. They have to keep in toe with the revelation of events as much as they can to ensure that they are on the right track committed to the cause of action. This does not dispute the fact that every project has an easy breakthrough; some are so difficult that when developers do not have faith, they heighten their chances of failing. In order to counteract such challenges, the developers have to come up with the best way of collaborating all the required plans to meet the specifications.

The enterprise architecture makes an effort to draw a technical roadmap that defines the support and evolution of the technicity of the organization. The roadmap enables the management to draw a good guideline to product management, which ensures that it meets the technical requirements. Additionally, it creates a common technical infrastructure in the production environment which is consistent.

It is very important to monitor the technical roadmap, which ensures that the existing IT infrastructure implements the future vision of the upcoming event. The infrastructure includes the network, servers, and software services. Additionally, it is wise to identify the infrastructure in which the organization operates and how they outsource the experts. Did they have to use external expertise or the internal expertise they already have within the organization? In most cases, the organization has a human resource department that establishes the data center through cloud technologies just like the way it is done in the external organization.

Moreover, some critical security issues that should be taken into consideration to ensure that the system is secure and sustainable. The management should be flexible and create a cost-saving strategy that eases the sophistication that may exist in the market. Outsourcing personnel from outside the country makes life more sophisticated, and it requires potential bottlenecks, which must be executed well.

Typically, the IT infrastructure builds a prolific solution to provide malleable solutions to the problems at hand. With softwarization, developers virtualize a defined data center where the code is mined from to ensure that they are incorporated into the system in the right manner. One should remember that DevOps is all about taking the risk of continuity where future is not guaranteed by the market or customers.

Risk aversion in an organization tends to affect different aspects of the DevOps development where the adoption of digital and innovation all rely on the risk involved. In this case, one should calculate risk accurately and know how to ensure that there is an achievable goal attained with low risk. Normally, one cannot always avoid risk; instead one should know how to manage the existing risks. Knowing what the risk entails and how to go over it is what matters to the organization. It is worth noting that not all risk is worth taking. Thus, it is imperative to analyze every risk with its consequences and benefits. Some risky businesses are greatly rewarding, and they can create a breakthrough in the business. However, those who normally play it safe usually end up losers in the business sector.

Therefore, one should embrace risk as it comes to ensure that the results are worthwhile. Critically, the risk depends on the company culture and how it rhymes with the existing environmental conditions. To ensure that one take good care of the project, one should take on small and lower reward-yielding projects. Such projects tend to possess less risk to the company, and they can prove to be the breakeven point of the organization. Moreover, precautions should be taken by the company to secure an insurance cover for the riskiest dealing, thus eliminating the chances of losing everything in a worst case scenario. There is a chance that the system can crash, leaving the company nonfunctional. Such instances should be anticipated before they occur. In such instances, the system maintainers should be updated about any glitches that may occur during the system's operation. In addition, the system's metric and time failure histories should be minimized to ensure that all the baseline measurements are as per the specifications. By doing so, the employees and the shareholders will be motivated since everyone desires an improved system that is efficient and effective for any duty. Moreover, one should prioritize and mitigate the kind of risk involved in a project before starting in any venture.

DevOps Improvement

Over the past few years, systems have been failing due to defaults in security, effectiveness, and efficiency. Due to these challenges, DevOps development has come up with an unique emphasis on how to improve the system to fuel quick releases, more collaborations, better quality, and greater efficiency for effective software. However, these efforts towards improving the system have created a strain on QA management arising from several process shifts while modifying the software. Though there are many challenges encountered by DevOps developers and the operation IT team towards modifying the software, practices have been put in place to ensure that there is an efficient and interactive interface that remains cost-effective.

Though there are some bottlenecks in the process which may render the process undeliverable, DevOps can still get away from systemic failure to make the software profitable and efficient for users. There is a way in which DevOps promotes knowledge and experience sharing to ensure that there is faster decision making, better overall quality, and conducive working environments for all employees, shareholders, and customers. To improve the system to its full responsive process, there are some of the factors taken into account, and I will try my best to explain them in layman's language for better understanding.

First and foremost, the company has to identify any bottlenecks that exist within the system. No matter how good the software may seem to be, there is always an issue when compared with other software, as trends continually develop and change in the market. During the DevOps development, there is a likelihood that developers are prone to encounter roadblocks arising from the emerging trends in the IT industry. In most cases, there is procedural inadequacy when it comes to completing the development circuit, employee inefficiency in carrying out expected tasks, and ineffective process development in line with requirements. In general, major bottlenecks in system development arise from the tech teams' inefficiency to meet the set standards.

In most cases, they are reluctant to ensure that the system is developed from the set codes to be adopted. Failure to create a concrete code leads to a leak in the security matters of the software. It makes software vulnerable to attack and unsustainable when released to the market. Also, there are communication barriers that make it hard for the DevOps to carry out tasks as required. To encounter that, most of the companies take the top-down approach to streamline the decision-making process which later ensures that the workflow is as per the standard set initially by the designers. For DevOps to streamline its adoption, it must ensure that the workflow and software development is efficient and effective for it to work well.

Moreover, the company will tend to have a setback when they adopt hybrid approaches as the basic way of encountering the bottlenecks in the industry. In that case, the DevOps cannot apply agile methodologies as the IT operations and engineering developers are kept at traditional silos. For the company to be highly productive, there is need for motivated staff at hand who can carry out their tasks efficiently towards automating things within the system by doing so; they propel chances of survival and prosperity of the software towards achieving its full potential.

Alternatively, one can place blame on the business objectives to keep up with the technological trends in the market. Just because one has to change the process does not mean that the overall goals of the whole process have to change as well. There is a likelihood that the change may bring new factors into play that may make the system better than the way it used to be initially. In fact, the organization's aspiration creates a great impact on ensuring that DevOps is successful through modification of various factors within the organization. The business objective determines the overall performance of the employees who later aid in the actualization of the whole process. A company should focus on prioritizing the backlog, which releases a consistent basis of feedback from the customers to ensure that the project is as per the requirement. By doing so, the development team is kept in check, and their efforts are appreciated towards making the DevOps a better system for software development. Nothing excites the employees like being appreciated, valued, and rewarded when they take on important tasks. It ensures that they are as per the specifications, requirement and developing objective.

Typically, the DevOps team should develop a clear oversight towards understanding the project's needs and creating more attention towards meeting the set requirements. For them to achieve that, they must monitor the key performance indicators of the company to ensure that it is up to date and under the system specifications. In such a case, DevOps has to develop necessary metrics to determine the stemming issues which may develop in the system. These metrics should relate to the lifeblood of the system to ensure that it is up to date and per the set requirements. By obtain such pieces of information, the company can identify weak points, and the various concepts needed to be corrected to ensure that the whole system is functioning as required. What is important is the availability of the information for informed decision-making process in the system. Since the entire business depends on the information made by the developers and the operation team, being informed about the emerging trends in the market ensures that the system is effective and up to the requirement to meet the set objectives of the company.

Ultimately, the organization can optimize the process by making it more efficient and effective by considering the containers in the system. The chances are high that the containers may not be the best solution to every setback encountered in the system development or service delivery and should be taken into consideration to ensure that the project is as per the set standard. Through this, DevOps can easily ensure that their project is as per the requirement and it meets the set goals and objectives through considering containers. It set the whole process apart by ensuring that the applications are more suitable and manageable by the developers.

DevOps Metric Practices

It is worth the effort to configure the DevOps challenges to be encountered by the metrics tracked. Most of the organization has different issues when it comes to deployment, which may lower the defect rate escape. In this case, we will place more focus on various challenges that require the use of metrics. Nevertheless, before that, one needs to know the initial intention of the whole system and how the DevOps ensure that metrics are utilized fully. One should take note that the main goal of DevOps is the quality, velocity, and efficiency of the application performance, and these should not be confused with anything else that does not add up to the healthy operation of the software system.

When aiming to ship code as fast as possible, one should consider how this can be done based on the product variety, risk tolerance, and the capability of the development team. Even if the metrics are not tracked around the velocity and quality, one should measure the efficiency and effectiveness of the whole system. However, there is a greater impact on caring about the quality all the time; it ensures that the production is as per the requirement and all the considerations are taken good care of at a given point of development.

Identifying the deployment size enables the organization to track down various features and stories as per the customer's specifications. Here, bugs are fixed, and some are deployed to other DevOps metrics, an act that ensures consistency in the process. It normally depends on many factors and not necessarily the work items of an individual at the workplace, which makes the whole process unique and effective. One should track down the development work which can be deployed in the system thus making it unique and viable at the same time.

Characteristically, one should deploy the frequency of the metrics in the system to ensure that things are as per the requirement of the whole process. Tracking down how often the deployment is done helps in developing a great DevOps system. The main aim of this process is to carry out more frequent deployment as much as possible to ensure that the software is set apart from any bugs that may hinder its effectiveness. By doing so, one can test and release the system to the market more often without encountering as many bottlenecks in the process. For this to be effective, one should consider counting non-production and production deployments separately. These processes ensure that there exists a frequent pre-production environment and QA analysis which makes the whole process important and effective throughout testing and bug-fixing in the system.

Another metric used in DevOps practices is the deployment time, which tracks how long it takes to complete a task. Time is a basic factor when it comes to any work being done, and it does not matter the type of task or work which is carried out. All that matters is the time taken by it to be complete. How often it is done and what is the rate of completion that ensures that it is done within a specified period. How does it feel to complete a task past the deadline? Is it reasonable to be late all the time and come up with varied excuses after missing important dates? By considering all these things, one can be in a position to realize the importance of time in any activity. Therefore, applications of the DevOps are subjected to the same principle. The Stackify tool is improvised in the system to deploy workers' roles, and it tracks down the rates of work per hour in the system. By doing so, the organization can easily detect any potential problem in the system which can lead to shutting down the whole process. By deploying this tool, it normally ensures that one can easily create room for adjustment by ensuring that the rate of completion is very fast.

DevOps metrics should be developed by ensuring that the shipping code is made quickly thus ensuring that the lead time is established. Typically, the lead time for a project can be simply be stated as the time between the starting point and the time it is deployed in the market. Normally, it helps one in determining the new work item to be established in due course. It determines how long the process takes until it reaches the production peak of development. It is very important in developing BizDevOps in the system.

Sometimes, having customer tickets can be the best or the worst application problem encountered in the system. The feedback received from the customers can make or ruin the business; thus, caution should be taken when using the customer ticket as the main metric of DevOps. No one intends to be a failure. For that reason, it can be detrimental if customers detect bugs in the system and can easily lead to the downfall of the company in the long run. On the other hand, positive reviews tend to create a positive impression about the product, and it helps in boosting the developer's morale to work harder and smarter towards improving the system. A quality performance is the greatest desire of the developers, and it provides a leeway towards accomplishing great things in the world today.

Furthermore, all these success rates can be geared by employing an automated test pass percentage in the system performance. It ensures that there is an increased velocity, which indicates that the team has fully utilized the functional testing required. One should note that DevOps highly relies on automation when tracking the automation test, which works best in any situation. One should take note of how the code change which may create a test break.

Additionally, it is worth the effort to take time to determine how often software defects occur and whether they are being found during the production or QA of the system. If the goal is to quickly ship out code, one should have confidence in the venture and take into consideration that there is a likelihood of getting software defects in the process, which should be executed well before establishing full response on the system. Creating a DevOps defect escape rate ensures that the metric track is monitored and all the defects are put under control. By doing so, one can easily track down the rate at which the defects get into production, and countermeasures are put in place to regulate or control the likely effects of such defects in the system.

DevOps Business Drivers

There are various business drivers which ensure that the whole system follows the set objective of the development. Mostly, cost reduction measures are taken into consideration to maximize the output and minimize the overhead inputs during production. In this case, some of the factors always considered by DevOps to reduce losses in the organization are necessary, and their impact highly affects the general appearance of the system. When software deliveries take too much time before they are marketed, there will definitely be an increased cost of delivery which will, in turn, cause an organization to experience losses. However, for this to be prevented, IT firms consider using DevOps team to ensure faster deliveries of software products within the specified timeline for effective production and software delivery. The team ensures that they gather much knowledge on functional skills to reduce dependency on people thereby limiting market delays. Besides, the management has come up with the best alternative of depending on people by incorporating automated system software, which ensures that all processes are executed without any delay or external hindrance.

Since DevOps possess a wider knowledge of functional skills in the IT environment, the tendency to increase agility will be adapted by the team to ensure that operational requirements are descriptively understood. The internal skills of the developers play a major role in this case thus making it more useful and necessary for expansion. However, the DevOps team will ensure a combination of Information Technology with strategic needs of the business with greater ability ,thereby experiencing higher levels of invention and innovation. By doing so, they facilitate faster responsiveness to ensure customer satisfaction and enabling the creation of news channels in the market. These practices usually promote proper coordination in IT firms, thereby increasing marginalization of the organization's profit and expansion necessary for growth. What else could a company admire more than the responsiveness to growth and profits achieved through proper management? This is the ideal motive behind any company in the world and a DevOps development team is not exceptional.

Critically, the team often elaborates on the improvement of the software's quality to minimize business and operational risks in an organization. The practice is mainly important in such a way that it enhances proper technical procedures when developing software to come up with the best and modern version of software delivery. It thereby increases the market demand of the software product and the profitability in IT firms that focuses on this practice. Moreover, it ensures that there is an effective and efficient use of the latest technology in the software when deriving the codes to be installed or automated for proper production.

Furthermore, these practices are identified with creating and designing model teams to enhance better collaboration within the IT staff to come up with effective software management. Most of the development team and the operations teams tend to be at heads due to diverse opinions that exist during production. At times, certain team wants their ideas to be implemented over that of other teams, which can create a conflict of interest in the company. By designing a creative model, the team can easily develop a suitable working environment between employees and employers within IT firms. Such practices aid in ensuring longer working periods due to better understanding among employers and employees in tech firms.

Due to a better understanding between workers and employers in tech firms, DevOps will assume responsibility for uniting IT firms and businesses. By doing so, the chances of triggering IT to become more responsive to the needs of the business so that business enterprises can, in turn, be more responsive to the market are heightened by the practice. In addition, it will enable better understanding of the market by IT firms because of wider knowledge and effective market research done by the DevOps team. To that extent, it helps in ensuring reliability of both the business enterprises and IT firms due to effective teamwork. Also, it will promote better feedback from both business leaders and IT firm leaders, certifying better software delivery in the market economy.

Another important business driver of the DevOps team is the improvement of mobile development by use of modernized software products, which have become more recognizable in the market economy. Unlike analog products, which are outdated, many IT consumers today want to purchase evolved mobile phones because of their trendy features, which make them attractive when conveying information. Who else does not want to keep up with the latest technology? The need to be valued, regarded highly and needed in the community crowd our mindset to the extent that we do not like to be left out in any technological development. If we cannot take part in production then we can take part in consumption as long as we get the association with the latest marker release. Most of the trendy features are characterized by modern mobile applications like Instagram, Twitter, Skype, Google, and many more others.

To ensure that all things are in order, the DevOps team often takes its time to conduct continuous experimentation, taking risks and deriving important lessons from their past failures to improve on new technology. Frequently, they master operational fields and new technological skills that enable the team to come up with new technological inventions. By doing so, developers can create more convenient and reliable software products that storm the market to create a long-lasting impact on the consumers.

DevOps Culture

DevOps culture is centered around different subcategories that consist of small and multi-disciplinary teams. These teams all work individually, but take collective responsibility and oversight over customers' reactions and experiences with their product, as the incentive behind a DevOps-minded production over a traditional one is the increased accessibility and communication between the client and the maker. Product delivery is the fundamental culture of a DevOps venture, which determines its success at the end of the day. They do not need to cope with the market pressure to keep up with production; all that matters is the value they create in the system towards customer satisfaction. Production is at the heart of a DevOps team.

In most cases, DevOps teams work by applying agile practices in the workplace. The company does so by placing their small teams on similarly small-minded projects. By structuring large and complex products in this manner, the organization is not only able to eliminate unnecessary bureaucracy and other time and profit-draining necessities, but it is also able to better focus on facilitating a helpful and enjoyable experience for the customer as developers, operations, and management are divided tasks in a manner that requires cooperation and team play above individual differentiation. Agile practices also create easier and less-cluttered avenues for advancement in the system, and as all members of the team are equally invested and involved, there is no finger-pointing or shifting of blame when things go wrong. They are all equally responsible and liable for any bugs or errors in the product. However, one may be obliged to encounter some defects which may arise, where team members are assigned the role to play concerning their field of specialization, thus eliminating sluggishness in the system.

Furthermore, DevOps teams are able to work efficiently because they utilize a concept known as a growth mindset. The growth mindset is evidence-based, much like the scientific method. DevOps teams control and direct their developmental approach by noting their goals, making explicit and implementable hypotheses to carry out such goals, and attempt to prove their claims. The results, and whether they are successful or not, are taken into consideration, and the process is repeated. During the testing process, DevOps teams use monitoring and telemetry to observe and collect evidence and results. The real-time response allowed by these methods streamline the development process.

DevOps teams are not constrained to predetermined roles. Instead, their day-to-day jobs and tasks are determined by team members' realistic capabilities. Why? The role is there in the system, but how one is committed to delivering is what determines the continued operation in such roles; thus, productivity is made important by the firm. Besides, the development and operational skills are included in the firm objective and task descriptions of the employees. Both teams are responsible for the functionality of the end product, not just the management. This means that developers care for the product not only in its developmental stages but afterwards as well. In a DevOps-created product, developers will oftentimes be on standby to troubleshoot any issues as they appear. The essential crux upon which DevOps is founded is communication, and they are centered on collaboration, which is both encouraged and harnessed by their culture. Therefore, DevOps culture enjoys a symbolic relationship with agile development, requiring more fluidity than rigid structures that previously pervaded in the IT arena.

Chapter Four:
DevOps Tools

There are a few common tools employed in the DevOps environment, and they range from continuous delivery tools to integration and deployment tools, which put more emphasis on the automation of the system. These tools encompass configuration management tests when the system is built, version control, and application deployment, which includes any monitoring tools. For that reason, there are various tools used to implement the different processes of the DevOps system such as product and quality testing, code creation, production, and others.

System Monitoring Tools

This has been a hot topic, and many tend to shy away from it due to its complexity. In particular, monitoring tools have a high degree of automation complexity necessary when establishing the infrastructure and tools used. From this perspective, an integrated set of DevOps tools has been established to monitor the system on how they function to improve the overall performance. These tools aim at improving the visibility and productivity of the entire system to establish cross-functional collaboration. Therefore, establishing the right tools is essential and necessary through developing discipline, culture, and practices that come with the entire process.

Typically, monitoring tools could be considered to be the essential information management guide to DevOps which ensures that the system performs optimally. Though there are different tools in the market that can be used to ensure that the system is up to date, it is functional, and it can also sustain all the activities which it does.

Tools like Nagios and Zabbix are some of the traditional ones incorporated in the system. These are open-source software, and though they are not well equipped to handle the diverse nature of DevOps that changes daily depending on market needs, they are still effective. In the case that one decides to use these monitoring tools, internal capabilities on the APIs should be extended on support the automating adaptation to configuration and changes to resource capacity.

There are also modern tools like Prometheus, Sensu, New Relic Infrastructure, and SysDig, which can be incorporated into the system to make it more viable and useful. All of these features monitor various computer resources, networks, storage availabilities, and inventories in the system. Moreover, DysDig and Prometheus are adopted for containers, which is very essential in the changing world infrastructure.

Companies like Amazon and Google usually use AWS, Cloudwatch, and stock drivers to ensure that operation is up to standards. These programs monitor productivity by watching the performance information of APIs. Though there are other forms of data transfer possibly enabled through CPU utilization or configured through notification alerts whenever the threshold is exceeded by the developer, it is worth noting that AWS user tends to inject their own metrics in the system to generate a great comprehensive analysis.

There is also an APM tool used in monitoring as the bottleneck target for the application framework. It allows the system to detect any defects that may exist in the system and deal with it appropriately. It is a unique tool compared to other tools used for monitoring the system functionality, and it enables one to create a good interface of the DevOps. On the other hand, there is a modern reigning market leader known as the New Relic which is installed for monitoring following a good reason. Precisely, it pinpoints the bottleneck in the system immediately it appears. Getting these kinds of tools ensure that there is no crackdown in the system and one can easily monitor everything going on in the system thus ensuring that the whole process is secure and up to date. Additionally, the use of AppDynamics has been integrated into the system to monitor various activities in the software functionality, which later determines the outcome of the DevOps. It also offers a clear view of the user transaction data through its performance of the metrics installed in the software.

Currently, there is great development in this technological error where tools like BigPanda and PagerDuty offer out-of-the-box integration solutions to achieve data aggregation. DevOps can easily view alerts in the system from this application, making it more useful and interesting. Moreover, these modern tools currently used in system monitoring are of great impact to the way DevOps are run to bring out the correlations between events.

It is important to remember that there are also other multiple systems integrated to modify the user's system of every organization. Most of these monitoring tools are displayed in big screens for easy analysis and verification of defaults which may occur in the system. Besides, there are ways in which alerts can view by the management efficiently with no much ado on the side of developers. The operation team may have peace of mind knowing full well that all their worries are taken care of by the monitoring tools installed in the system.

Network Tools

Since the DevOps software development is mainly concerned with communication, a collaboration between products and management, the software is essential for its operations professionals. From this perspective, there are management tools that can be used to make the whole process more successful.

Git is extensively used and modified across the software industry as a Source Code Management (SCM) tool by DevOps. It is commonly preferred by most of the developers and remote teams due to its nature as a source contributor due the fact that it provides open-source progress tracking on work development. Moreover, many software companies use it to create separate branches whereby they come up with new features as a great tool for experimentation. GitHub and Bitbucket are regarded as the best two online Git Repos hosting services developed by DevOps.

Furthermore, Jenkins, who is an automation tool for many software development teams provides automation platform necessary at different levels in pipeline delivery. Since it provides more than 1000 plugins in the current software industry, it became a popular tool in the software ecosystem. It is simple, to begin with, Jenkins as it runs out-the-box on Windows, Mac OS, and Linux, and it can easily be installed with Docker. Its server can be configured and set up through a web interface, and first-time users have the easy option to install it with commonly used plugins. In that case, it provides easy deployment, and the creation of new codes can be done as fast as possible when incorporated correctly. Moreover, it fosters the effective measurement of success in each step of a pipeline delivery. Even though some complain about Jenkins's "ugly" and non-intuitive UI, a software developer can still find everything they want using this tool without a problem.

Another CI/CD solution tool with similar characteristics to Jenkins is Bamboo due to the fact that both can be used for automation of delivery pipeline, from build to deployment. The difference that exists between Bamboo and Jenkins as a software tool is that Bamboo comes with a price tag while Jenkins is open-source. So choosing a proprietary software depends entirely on the user's budget and goals. The reason why Bamboo has fewer plugins, which number only 100 in comparison to Jenkins 1000+, is that it has many pre-built functionalities that have to be manually set up in Jenkins. Besides, Bamboo allows for easy access to built-in Git and mercurial branching workflows and software test environments because of its seamless combination with other Atlassian products like Jira and Bitbucket. So it is quite evident that Bamboo can save developers a lot of configuration time as it also brings about a more intuitive UI consisting of tips, auto-completion, and other attractive software characteristics, thus making many software developers prefer it over Jenkins.

The number one container platform is Docker since its successive launch in 2013, and it is still experiencing continuous improvement as a widely-recognized tool in the software industry. Containerization has been made popular in the highly developing technology world by Docker because it allows for easy distribution of development and quick automation of deployment of software apps. Easy separation of applications into separate containers is made possible by Docker, enabling them to become more portable and more secure. Docker containers can serve as substitutes for virtual machines such as Virtual Box. Dependency management is limited when Docker is used as a software tool because dependencies can be packaged within the app's container and ship the whole thing as an independent unit allowing developers to run the app any machine or platform without any difficulty. Docker, Jenkins, and Bamboo, if combined and used together with one of these automation servers can enable further improvement in the developer's delivery workflow. Cloud computing is also one of the greatest characteristics of Docker as a software tool making the major reason why cloud providers such as AWS and Google Cloud added support to Docker as it greatly simplifies the task of cloud migration.

Kubernetes is a container orchestration platform that was invented by a couple of Google engineers who were more interested in finding the solution of managing containers at scale. Though it is still new in the software industry as it was launched in 2005, it works perfectly well with Docker or any of its substitutes. Easy automation of the distribution and scheduling of containers across the whole cluster is made possible by Kubernetes because it can be deployed to a cluster of computers so that users do not have to tie their containerized apps to a single machine. Its content is made up of one master and several worker nodes, and it pays attention to almost everything. Implementation of predefined rules is made by the master node and distributes the containers to the worker nodes Redeployment is made necessary by Kubernetes if it notices that a worker node is down.

Puppet Enterprise allows for convenient management of developers' infrastructure as code because as it automates infrastructure management, developers can deliver software faster and more securely. For smaller projects, a puppet will provide developers with an open-source tool because it is a cross-platform configuration management platform that enables developers to focus more on their software management skills thereby improving quality in software deliveries. When dealing with a larger infrastructure, Puppet Enterprise will be valuable with extra characteristics such as Real-time reports, Role-based access control, and Node management. Easy management of multiple teams and thousands of resources is possible with Puppet Enterprise because it will automatically understand relationships within a given infrastructure, and will handle failures effectively because it also understands how to deal with dependencies. It can easily integrate with many popular DevOps tools because it contains more than 5000 modules that can assist in skipping failed configuration thereby making it convenient as the best DevOps tool in terms of management strategies.

Raygun as a software tool will help accurately diagnose performance issues and track them back to the exact line of code, function, or API call. It can easily detect priority issues, thereby creating effective solutions for software problems. Raygun brings Development and Operations together by providing a single source of truth for the entire team, the cause of inaccuracies, and performance problems because it can automatically link errors back to the source code.

Log Monitoring

Before choosing any log monitoring tools, there are several factors to consider, including the functionality of these tools. There has recently been greater interest and focus on creating log management tools trained with machine learning. There is a range of features that are integrated into the system requirement, which ensures that the system is stable and sustainable to end users.

These may include the range and scalability of the tools to be incorporated in the system, which covers the product user expands in which the DevOps source of logs is monitored. One should always take note that the logging tool has to collect and manage all the logs from the system component through the server monitoring enabled logs. Since access is provided from a central location, there is a need to create speed from all the logging tools used in DevOps. Therefore, there is a need to keep an eye on the process when seeking different solutions to the system processes at hand.

On the other hand, one may look for advanced aggregation capability when selecting suitable log tools to be used in monitoring the system. In most cases, one can be overwhelmed with unnecessary data collected during logging time. When looking for a good aggregation tool, software which should be considered are those who have shared characteristics that ensure that log origin in servers, database, devices, and applications are free from error regardless of the user's actions. Moreover, there is the need to observe the intelligent pattern recognition in log monitoring tools proposed by the developers. To establish an intelligent pattern on DevOps, machine learning on the contemporary logging tools must be observed. The organization needs to create such chances for people to have great knowledge of machine learning promotes more knowledge on what to do and how to do it where DevOps is concerned. In this case, there is a need to learn the standard log syntaxes used on various systems for a much analysis needed by the developers and the operation team. It gives a platform on how the logs look like and how they are being incorporated into the system.

In DevOps log monitoring, there have been open-source tools that have been integrated into DevOps software to deliver efficiency of the application through logging tools. When monitoring the logs of the DevOps system, some tools should be incorporated into the system to make it more efficient and up to the requirement of the users. In this case, monitoring cloud platforms by the use of application components for processing and analyzing logs are made essential to make it more stable. Moreover, the availability of the application can be backed with other forms of logs, which make it useful.

The fact that the proprietary logging and other monitoring solutions have to remain expensive in the market, much focus has been shifted to targeted tasks whereby container cluster monitoring have been integrated to make it perfect. These tools prove to be holistic alerting and monitoring toolkits, which is responsible for creating a multi-dimensional data collection and other querying amenities.

According to Linux foundation in their guide release report on open cloud trends that are used to modify the system, the guide expounded on the third party annual report with a comprehensive state of cloud computing on logs. They incorporate the tools necessary for open cloud computing, whereby the logging monitoring is comprehensively expounded. Besides, the report entails the download aggregates necessary for analyzing the whole process thus making it a global community that illustrates different containers, monitoring and sharpening cloud computing system. From the report, one can easily access links for the descriptions of the projects intended to create a conducive environment for better performance. All these are enhanced through log monitoring, which is put in place to guide the initiator of the project and the developing team from slide back in the system. No one likes to fail, and when it comes to DevOps development, creating a sustaining application is important since it enables one to have full control of the software.

There is the continued use of Fluentd as a source of data collection tool on the logs made in the system with the aid of unified logging layer. The tool is modified in such a way that it incorporates JSON facets of processing log data through buffering, filtering, and outputting logs to other multiple destinations. Besides, such achievements in the system are enhanced through fluentd on the GitHub system. Contrary to that, most of the developers have found a way of using a container cluster for monitoring the performance using analysis tool in kubernetes. The tool supports kubernetes well, and it also enables CoreOS to operate natively, whereby the adaptation is made possible through the use of OpenShift system of the DevOps.

To understand how all these things are made possible, no need to look far; just search for an expert who understands it well. Technology is complex, and I do not expect everyone to grasp everything am talking about in DevOps, but it is important in the current technological landscape to, at the minimum, understand the main concepts behind the tool. Most of the time, people will lose attention whenever DevOps practices and tools are mentioned; the concept is much more important to those who have developed an interest in technology. How else can one do without technology in this modern world where everything is modified by humans to fit the need? Personally, I spend much of my time on the internet, searching for various features that need improvement. From the research I have done, it is very obvious that most of the influx DB technology is developed through the use of Google Cloud monitoring and logging, Grafana, Riemann, Hawkular and Kafka.

Additionally, the use of Logstash, which is an open-source to data pipeline, enables one to process logs and event data very fast. It is enabled through the use of data from a variety of systems, which made it convenient and effective to process data in the system. Logstash tool is very interesting, and the use of plugins make it more convenient in connecting variety of sources and stream of data which ensures that the central analytic system is streamlined to meet the specifications and the software requirement.

There is also a Prometheus system used by most of the applications in monitoring and as an alerting toolkit in the SoundCloud. In this case, a cloud-native computing foundation has come up with different consolidated codes to make the whole system work. Recently, the software has been configured to fit the machine-centric and micro service architectures in such a way that it creates a multi-dimensional data whenever there is a need for data collection and querying.

Deployment and Configuration Tools

DevOps is indeed evolving, and each day it is gaining popularity among people in the world. Many organizations have gained the traction of this software, which enables them to produce efficient applications and increase product sales in the market. Moreover, this has been enabled through core values like automation, measurement, and sharing towards the organization's influence. In this case, one can note that culture of the DevOps is strategically used to bring people and processes together in order to carry out certain tasks. Specifically, culture of DevOps is to develop the system by combining different factors to make the whole process work.

On the other hand, automation is used to create a fabric for the DevOps system which eases the culture in the organization while measurements aid the improvement essential where DevOps is concerned. However, the last part, sharing, closes the whole deal as it enables the feedback from all other application tools. The customer's review must be considered more so where decision making is required.

Similarly, DevOps have the greatest concept which supports the whole process where everything can be remotely managed by network, servers, log files, application configuration via code. These code control also help the developers to automate various tests in the system, create database, and deployment process through a cool running of the software.

Let us now shift our focus on deployment and configuration tools, which is the major concept of this section. Here, one must know that the configuration management tools are very important just like the deployment tools used in the DevOps system. It creates best application practices necessary for developing it into full use to the concerned parties.

Through manipulating simple configuration files, most of the DevOps team can employ the use of the best development practices, which may include version control, testing, and kind of various deployments incorporated with design patterns. By the use of code, the developers can manage infrastructure, automate the system and create a viable application for users in the market.

Moreover, by the use of configuration deployment and configuration tools, the developers can easily change the deployment platform to be faster, scalable, repeatable, and predictable in order to maintain the desire for state. So the assets are set to work by the desired state that is transitioning by the other parties in the process. This kind of configuration cannot be achieved without considering some of the advantages associated with it.

For the tools to be useful and up to the task requirement, there must be adherence to coding convenience, and all other factors are catered for before configuration into the system. By doing so, the developers can easily navigate the code used and make fine adjustments whenever required or when need arise for upgrading. No system is perfect, and at one point or another, there arises the need for improvement and adjustments which must be made by the developers to fit the customers' needs derived from the feedback. In such a case, one is required to tread softly and observe all the obstacles that may arise in the course of development. However, the idempotency of the codes must be kept clean during the adjustments. This is to means that all the code should remain ii tacked as long as it is in use. It does not matter how many times the code has been executed; it must remain the same for future development, which may mean upgrading the system. In case one interferes with the code, future development may be made difficult, and sometimes one will derive them from somewhere else thus creating a new avenue for new DevOps creation. Similarly, a distribution design should be configured in the system to enable developers and DevOps operation teams to manage remote servers.

Pull models are used by some configuration management tools in the system as agent servers in the central repository purpose. Though there are a variety of configuration tools used by the DevOps to manage the software, and some of the features truly make it a great situation for others that are involved in the making. Therefore, there is a need for identifying and analyzing these deployment and configuration tools in full. In this case, the information obtained is based on the tools software repositories and various websites that provide the required information.

I will consider Ansible to be the most preferred tool used in IT automation since it makes the application more simple and easy to deploy. It is most suitable in situations where regular writing of scripts or custom code is not necessarily needed to deploy code. It updates the system with an automated language approach, which can be easily comprehended by anyone who cares to learn about the code used in the application. By doing so, there is no agent for installing a remote system in the software, and the information is readily available in Github repository, documentation done by the developers, and the community in which the system is developed.

Ansible stands out due to its features, which makes it the favorite of many developers and users around the world. One can use this tool to execute various tasks in the application ranging from matching the command in different servers at the same time using it at one point end. The tool automates tasks by the use of "playbooks" which are written in YAML file. The playbook facilitates communication among the team members and non-technical experts in the organization. The most important aspect of this tool is that it is simple to use, easy to read, and gentle to handle by anyone in the team though there is need for ansible tool to be combined with other tools to create a central control process.

Alternatively, one can use CFEngine as a configuration and deployment tool in DevOps development and management. Its main function in the system is to maintain and create a configuration avenue necessary in large scale computer sustenance. Just a brief history and working knowledge of CFEngine can be of much importance to some people, if not all, that may care to know much about the revelation of the tool. It was discovered by Mark Burges back in 1993 in an attempt to automate configuration management of the system. The reason behind the discovery was to deal with the entropy bugs in the computer system and to ensure that the convergence is unique and up to the desired state of the configured system. From his research, he proposes a promise theory which was later reinvented in 2004 by the cooperation between agents in the business.

Currently, the use of this promise agent theory has been put in place in such a way that it enables the running servers to pull the configuration in the system, which makes everything better at the end of the day. Though it requires some expert knowledge and for it to be integrated into the system without much ado or error there are some aspects which may cause the system to fail during installation which must be avoided at all cost. Therefore, it is best suited for the experts in the IT industry or those who have used it severely and have learn the unique features to look for during installation.

Additionally, one can intend to use a system integration framework to deploy and configure different applications in the system. Also, it is suitable for creating a platform for configuration management and installation in the entire infrastructure at hand. Its code is written in Ruby in order to keep the system running and updated all the time. The recipe used primarily describes all the series of resources that should be updated in the system, and more importantly, chef can easily run the client mode through a standout configuration called chef-solo. Due to all these factors, one should not forget that it has a great integration, which is a major cloud provider which automatically configure new machines. One should remember that chef has a solid user base which provides a solid full toolset built from different technical background for proper support and understanding of the application.

Chapter Five:
Adopting DevOps

When it comes to adopting DevOps, one should consider the most optimal way to lead to rapid agility and deliverable services to potential customers in the market. In doing so, quality should not be compromised at all costs, though such a conviction stands out as one of the greatest challenges in the industry. According to many IT leaders in the market, implementing DevOps in practice can be the most useful aspect of accelerating software release with minimal complications while delivering a quality application for use. If one is considering moving in on the DevOps delivery model, several key approaches must first be taken into consideration.

First and foremost, one should embrace the DevOps mindset to stand apart from the rest. Switching to DevOps does not happen overnight, and one should be prepared for the hurdles involved in the development process. It is important to take the time and resources needed for such a feat into consideration. Understanding the gist of achieving the set goal matters a lot where DevOps development is concerned as well. The entire organization should have a common focus towards realizing the goal set at the beginning so that every member of the firm can work to achieve it in the end product. There are specific business needs that must be met, and the willingness to change along with any inevitable changes that show up during development must be adhered to anytime they crop in as the process go by in the organization.

The most prudent way to go about the process is to identify the current application streams that determine the resources needed during the development of the DevOps. These involve identifying series of activities necessary for moving the products from the initial development stages to the production level by understanding that the delivery process involves many constraints on the developer's part and seeing that there is a need to study the whole situation carefully. The bottlenecks, challenges, and unpleasant activities in the process enable the worker to identify and stick to what they are supposed to do or identify the best alternative to concentrate on during development. Besides, the organization only needs to concentrate on some activities which need development by improving it to a desirable nature at the end.

However, it is important to also identify current ineffective delivery areas that need to be improved as the best way of capitalizing on the opportunity at hand. To do so, one needs to experiment with the whole process and identify different faults that may exist. After identifying potential issues, concentrate on the most critical fault first. Then, follow up with the best time to execute the activity to accomplish the best delivery. There may be times where one needs to ask questions on what should be done, when to do them, and why the activity has to be carried out by the company. In such cases, the team must ponder the matter at hand and brainstorm the best alternative choices so that the end product is one of quality and usefulness. Sometimes there is a need to investigate the whole process and assemble all the resources needed along with necessary inputs that should be taken into consideration. Remember that the planning process must be intense in such a way that nothing is left out during the planning process. By doing so, all the factors are likely to be considered, and cost of carrying out is estimated according to the budget. Sometimes it hurts when an activity starts without clear plans on how to accomplish or finish it in the long run. As always, managing things beyond the scope of plan is difficult and even more so when all the other activities are on schedule. However, by thoroughly considering the business value, efficiency, and effectiveness of the entire process, the planning becomes very easy, and that determines the entirety's success.

Within the industry, DevOps is often taken as synonymous with automation, but there is quite a difference in that automation is used to accelerate the manual process of the system, in other words the DevOps system. It is worth noting that DevOps primary concern is with collaboration and communication. These factors are catered for in software development of delivery, testing, and operation processes which make the system yield a desirable benefit for the organization.

After identifying the potential bottlenecks, one needs to make the most desirable metrics to be adopted in developing DevOps. During the adoption of DevOps, most people tend to overlook the right metric to be used in recording and tracking the progress, though such a tool is critical for successful adoption of the method. In this case, one should adopt the right baseline DevOps metric as early as possible and ensure that a key factor is considered during the adoption process to make it valuable and necessary. It can be demonstrated in the process of estimating the business benefits that would be earned in the long run.

One essential DevOps metric to be considered is the production failure rate, which can determine how often the system fails and whether failure occurs during fixed periods. From this perspective, one can anticipate any future failure in the system and plan for it in advance. What matters is that those involved know about such events occurring, and if so, they will not be taken by surprise when it eventually occurs. Also, determine the meantime, or the time the application will take, to recover. This is very important more so when it comes to DevOps adoption where the application code should not be complicated to hinder the recovery process. Besides, there is an average lead time, which has to be taken into consideration during DevOps adoption. Here, one determines the requirement of developing the whole process like the sources to be delivered, built and tested on deploy into production of the DevOps. Moreover, there is a need to determine the deployment speed where the version speed is estimated on the rate at which it can deliver. That should be integrated with the frequency of deployment, which is the release of the candidate test that concerns the production staging and production environment. Also, the meantime to production is highly considered during DevOps adoption, along with the time needed before new code committed in the production can yield results. One must be aware of what it takes for the whole process to be successful.

All the above metrics cannot limit one from exploring more since there is still much to be considered in the adoption process. There are many metrics to consider, but one should be careful not to collect undesirable metrics unsuitable for the adoption. Metrics that look impressive but not benefit the business should be avoided by all means. While these metrics may bolster outsiders' view of the team, the numbers are of little or no benefit to the business in the long run. In fact, they may detract from the business by wasting valuable time and resources on collecting these metrics instead of addressing other, more vital concerns.

It is nevertheless important to look at the metrics and consider the relevant ones in deeper detail in such a way that the DevOps's goals are in line with the metric incorporated. Essentially, it is good to share the DevOps goals to align them with the system development progress, which enhances an easy adoption process. The metric dashboard should be set in such a way that it displays the current situation which needs to be improved for it to be adaptable. Even in other instances, one is rewarded according to what they already have and the progress they need to make out of the existing situation at hand. With complete transparency of the metrics, developers are likely to achieve the set goal of the process within the timeline.

Additionally, the developers are required to understand and address the unique needs of the DevOps for it to be adopted. Similar to how the sellers of DevOps products need to know the specifications and technicalities of the product, the developers have to see that it fits all their needs. Every DevOps has specifications which make it unique and valuable for adoption. What needs to be analyzed is how it fits the need of a specific application and the important aspects to be looked at during its implementation. One cannot just drop an automated tool into the system and hire a self-proclaimed engineer to manage it without further investigation of what is required in the system adoption. Doing so would be insensitive and contrary to the technology fraternity.

Moreover, there should always be a specific business culture and journey to be followed to the letter during the adoption of a suitable DevOps to be employed in the system. Hence, there are always things or features that must match the need of the business for it to be profitable and desirable to the general public. How else can one adopt features which cannot help the system towards achieving set objectives of the organization? Consider a situation where customers do not like the business model used to deliver products. Most likely they will shy away from these products and opt to use competitors' products instead, incurring losses. No matter how unique the process is or tailor-made for a specific purpose, the customers' needs and wishes must be given priority at all levels of production. For instance, customers will not be happy if there are twenty mandatory system updates, no matter the intention triggering such action. The company should instead focus on improving the usability, security, and other essential aspects of developing the DevOps system.

Also, adopting the iterative can start the whole process without causing issues. It is important to remember that during the initial stages of DevOps adoption, one should avoid an enterprise-wide reconfiguration. Instead, one should identify the pivotal applications necessary for running the software and apply the method to those areas first. Therefore, there is a need to examine cross-functional DevOps strategies like tests, developments, and operations to determine the need and the constraints of their existence in the system. These are crucial in creating deployment pipelines that can address the process—challenges that may be hard to handle. For that reason, one should measure the progress, wash, rinse, and success where the whole process should be repeated to arrive at the best solution.

Typically, one should consider the main value stream constraint in the system, which is likely to cause the greatest impact on the business. In most cases, such constraints can easily be solved in the system making it less destructive to the whole development process, though there are some who normally take much time to be resolved leading to high vulnerability of the system. It is prudent to adopt systems that can be easily changed and fine tuned in such a way that the whole process is made available for use. One will tend to go through some of the iterations to build confidence in the system on how they work, and use various features to improve the whole process in such a way that there is no loss incurred during development. For that reason, there is built-in confidence for the parties involved and enhanced expansion of other projects. Moreover, there is a chance that one should make progress on the metrics used in such a way that there is an improved quality of delivery and software modification.

In this case, it is important to ensure that the influencers involved in the process are liable for their actions and that the respective team members are made aware of their actions. Besides, the expert's experience should not be locked up or constricted to a given set of principles that does not give room for expansion or is not up to the wellbeing of the whole process.

For those who are about to begin the DevOps journey, it is advisable to start from the delivery process then to production afterward. The development of the DevOps is made in such a way that its continuation depends on the initial stages. It has to graduate from one level to another for it to be more stable and desirable to be adopted by the developers of the software when the time is ripe. The property management and other management strategies are implemented in a unique way that enables it to have a downstream of the future process.

Furthermore, one can truly apply automation, which is the cornerstone for accelerating the adoption and delivery processes. There is a way of creating a conducive environment fit for all the developments, infrastructures, configurations, and necessary platforms needed to enhance a great improvement in the testing process during DevOps adoption. Most of these adoption processes should be in the form of defined written in code configured for the whole software development. Moreover, something like automation tools should be time-intensive and thoroughly run in the application though they are prone to error; one should take care of all the implications which come with it. By doing so, one can quickly benefit the team whereby the delivery times are highly reduced, and the repeatability of the adoption process is highly increased, thus eliminating any configuration drift that potentially exists in the system.

Standardizing the approach for automation should be given the top priority since it ensures that DevOps QA are adopted in the program development, and there is a common frame of reference that exists among the developers who communicate using common code language. Besides, it is important for one to adopt the use of software engineering best practices for DevOps automation. The quality of the application should match that of the automation used in the system.

Ultimately, there is awareness about the nature of DevOps that it cannot be bought by anyone or bolted or in a simpler way; it can only be achieved through the development of the software system. Though it normally takes time and there are many challenges along the way which must be incurred in order to realize its full potential and capability enhanced.

Reasons for Adopting DevOps Culture

Digitization is taking over the world, and many industries are on their way to adopting the digital or automation method of service delivery. For this reason, there has been an increase of unparalleled demand for companies to experiment, innovate, and deliver a faster software system to take care of the prevailing tasks in the market. There is a desire to increase the agility and speed of the application performance which has become the survival skill in technology industries. Nowadays industries strive to adopt a more efficient, effective and flexible approach for software delivery, which eliminates barriers that may exist and promotes dependencies between development and operations.

Naturally, the DevOps team environment gives rise to responsibility for delivering great features, which creates stability in the system. These development team not only creates code that runs on the applications, but they also create room for advancement and improvement of the system, which is essential to every organization. One cannot just build a code that is not flexible to changes and the complexity of the technology in the world today. There must be a balanced room that is created by both teams to build insight and visibility of the application performance.

Therefore, it is important to analyze the importance of adopting DevOps system in the organization to get a clear view of events and operations. These reasons should be triggered in such a way that they support the customer's experience and expectations. In order to keep pace with the market demand, the operation and development team must adopt different strategies to create a competitive advantage through a test, deploy, build, and release of suitable software in an ever-faster cycle.

Acceleration innovation should be adopted much faster to help the development team and integrated operation team to create and deploy a DevOps system much rapidly. It is vital to notice that most of the business today depends on the ability to create and innovate in order to compete fairly in the market. This can be attributed to change complexity, which exists, and it forces innovators to catch up with the system development. Therefore, DevOps engineers are in a position to take advantage of the developing issues in the world today where the performance of data is quickly modified to fit the prevailing market demand. The impact of the application change ensures that the developers can code the data effectively thus ensuring stability of the system. Besides, the software tends to fix faster, and the developer only needs to check the current situation of the system for modification.

The other reason for adopting DevOps is because of its improved collaboration nature. Instead of focusing on eliminating the existing difference between the disciplines for its development, DevOps only promise to build bridges and creates a system where they can work together for the betterment of the whole process. From this perspective, software development culture can focus on working together to create the best application for their customers and not on internal competition or any purported disparity. The main agenda is to research, innovate, and improve the system for the betterment of the organization. One can use a code today to develop a system but later realize that there is a better way of modifying the code to fit the need and that usually requires innovativeness on the developer's part. In this industry, the focus is on continuous achievement and not an individual gain that may be created to combat competition. Rather it is not a matter of tossing application code and hoping for things to work out with the best interest of the developers. Team members seem to embrace the environment in which they work and the interaction involved when creating a DevOps software.

Also, there is increased efficiency, which makes DevOps suitable for adoption. These are enhanced through automated tools and standardized production platforms created by the development and operation team. Moreover, there are best practices put in place to aid the deployment and delivery tools more predictable that the IT team can easily do the tasks repetitively. These are carried out with automated testing tools that ensure that integration processes are complete, and the developers have created an effort to avoid frittering away codes. Besides, the acceleration and development platforms of DevOps offer many other opportunities which aim at improving the efficiency of the system. Some of these opportunities are scalable infrastructure, which is a cloud-based solution to DevOps. The scalable infrastructure aim at creating testing speed and deployment process, which increase the access to hardware resources. Additionally, the compilation and development tools are integrated into the system to shorten the development cycle while, on the other hand increasing the delivery process of the products. These can be supported with continuous delivery workflow witnessed in DevOps to create a frequent software release to the world today.

DevOps are associated with a reduced failure approach, which is enhanced through a shorter development cycle, which promotes frequent code release. With great modular implementation, there is a likelihood that there is a problem in configuration, application code, and infrastructure, which are executed by the DevOps. The fact that the DevOps tend to engage members in the life cycle of the application makes it more admirable, and the resulting development gives rise to high-quality code for the system. However, there are fewer fixes that are required by the developers to make the whole process to be realistic. As depicted in the recent report about DevOps adoption, it was established that organizations that have adopted the DevOps culture into their system are 60 times less likely to experience any failure as compared to other firms that have not consider it. From this research, one can conclude that DevOps is safer for use and every organization should look into ways of adopting it for system efficiency. By implementing devops approach, organization can be assured that their system is safe from fraud, and any other intrusion which may arise from hawking attempt due to its stability.

Critically, DevOps adoption into the system accelerates the recovery time from the bugs and malfunction of the system. The deployment process is primarily isolated to the target, and it has an easy spot that can be fixed faster due to its easy implementation nature. The only thing that the team needs to do is to check the latest code and update the system accordingly whereby issues arising are updated in time thus reducing the software risk. In this case, the resolution time is faster since it has a responsible troubleshooting capability that stands out for itself. In fact, there is a high recovery of DevOps failure which has been witnessed in the world today.

Ultimately, there is an increased satisfaction realized by the use of DevOps. Instead of power or rule-based culture, DevOps has been established to promote more performance-based environments in the software industry. Due to that, there is increased risk-sharing which has reduced the bureaucratic obstacles that previously existed in the software industry. As a result, there has been a more content and productive workforce that dominates the market currently, and this workforce helps boost business performance. The developers usually prefer to work in DevOps environments due to effectiveness and efficiency of the team who work towards achieving a common goal with selfless interest on personal gain. Through that, the engineers and the developers can fit well in the system since their roles are well defined according to the need they are supposed to satisfy. Remember that they are available on demand and when the role is well-defined, they are likely to spend less time at the project and at the same time, yield a greater result.

Teamwork also plays a crucial role in ensuring that all the resources for development and operation are within their reach. The software delivery is much important and essential in today's digital age where everything is digitized to meet the human need or market demand. Since personal effort cannot meet all the human needs, there has been a situation where the automation is involved in the whole process to make things work effectively thus creating the need for DevOps software. It is this software that accelerates the market service and rolls out features that are effective and efficient. Moreover, it is not just a simple process that can be implemented overnight by the developers; it requires time and resources for it to be implemented to achieve its full delivery, and when done correctly, it pays the highest return.

DevOps Adoption Hurdles

Despite the breakthrough in IT maturity in the world today, most of the organizations still find it hard to embrace DevOps practices. According to Forrester's research, 50 percent of organizations are still testing the efficacy and usefulness of this concept, while only 13 percent have adopted and implemented this technology milestone in their software system. On the contrary, 9 percent of companies still have no plans of adopting DevOps practices. Moreover, there is more theory behind the slow uptake of DevOps in the world which proves to justify different technological challenges faced by the DevOps development in the world today.

Analytically, some experts depict that the application development has been made disperse by different agencies that exist in the industry while the infrastructure is owned by the commonwealth technology office. For that reason, silos have developed, and for DevOps to work, these restrictions must be aborted. On top of that, there is a broad array of systems that have made it difficult to adopt whereby the automation and continuous processes are made difficult for DevOps to work efficiently. Besides, the skills to support the full development of DevOps are not readily available in the state, creating the reluctance of application adoption in most industries. The organizations need to employ experts who can be responsible for the development of the DevOps system to its full utilization. It wise to note that every technological advancement needs an expert who would be responsible for its operation in the organization. In this case, many organizations find it difficult to employ suitable personnel for such tasks, making it more difficult to adopt such a system.

Technically, there have been pangs of culture change witnessed in DevOps adoption where most of the firms used the same principle. This principle has shorter and tighter feedback loops and weak usability testing. There is a high probability that most of these departments have not embraced DevOps shops. There is a need for a cultural shift, which arises from the way these departments operate, and this cannot be forced overnight. The development should be exercised over a given period, making it adaptable with the existing culture in the organization. Even though there is a need to devolve in DevOps application, it requires time to mature. It is very important to get over the IT system in such a way that all the modifications are made available. If so, one can access all that is required, but all these cannot be reached in the DevOps system, leading to delay in its adoption. For one to achieve these, one will have to revert to the right approach.

People-related issues have been identified as the major barrier to DevOps adoption. These barriers range from limited budget, diverse culture, and lacking IT skill sets. The only thing that can make transfer successful is when the company has no challenges in adopting the system. Moreover, these challenges seem to be more diverse for most people to handle and this makes it an expensive venture for most of the companies. But organizations do not always stick to traditional technology because of budgeting issues. Some stick to that old technology to retain the clients and make things possible for the developers. The idea of DevOps normally does not appeal to every company, and some only intend to use it partially, not as the main technological software in the organization. Due to this fact, the organization can be forced to bring along support who can understand the DevOps concept to ease the process of service delivery. There is a critical transformation tool that must be considered by the organization to ensure that all these challenges are taken care of within the timeline.

A fundamental rethinking on how the system works is taken into consideration, and to some extent, people create a business-oriented atmosphere where all the software application is analyzed. By doing so, there are resources committed to the task, which may make it a more expensive task to carry out. Creating the most effective and efficient venture ensures that all the development of DevOps is eased by the organization. Hence, chances are heightened for its adoption. However, there are groups within the organization that are allergic to change, and they always insist that the firm should always stick to traditional technology where there is no automation.

Apart from the culture, which is the basis for DevOps development, a continuous process of DevOps development creates a delivery platform for adoption. It is a slow process, and sometimes organizations may prefer a faster system where they can automate things quickly and efficiently without much ado in the process. In such cases, the adoption of the application becomes difficult. The organization would have to employ external expertise to monitor the functionality of the system along with the engineers to create the best platform for the DevOps and the general operation team. Therefore, with a short timeline for adoption, all these resources cannot be accessed by the management within the timeline limit. Whatever is good must be pursued by an entrepreneur who deserve to get something good out of the deal. Moreover, there is a possibility that most of the organizations will prefer to use the old technology to replace the current need which may involve much spending on the system.

Technically, the government-sponsored firms are prone to create a competitive advantage in the market, which may not be readily available in some of the industries across the world. The monopolistic legacy created by these enterprises makes it very difficult for others to catch up with the market trend. Remember that these sponsored enterprises usually receive support from the government to cater to the production cost while other firms may only finance their ventures through their earnings, a method that proves to be much more expensive in the long run. Self-sponsored industries tend to incur losses at the end of the day due to high trading costs, which they may experience during DevOps development and adoption. Due to that, they are inclined to shy away from DevOps adoption and opt for another cheap alternative in the market.

Signs That an Organization Is Not Ready for DevOps

Currently, DevOps is changing the way organizations operate, perform, and deliver on software necessary for their full utilization of resources. Most of the time, organizations are struggling to stand up on their own with the existing traditional technology, which tends to be outdated and ineffective thus creating inefficiency. Therefore, there are some signs which show that the organization is not yet ready for transformation through the new technology trend, DevOps, in their operation.

Whereas some organizations treat DevOps as the new trend in the market to justify their attention and any expenses spent on it, others still find it hard to adopt DevOps. These companies tend to maintain the traditional silos that they can still build or tack on without hustle at their part. All they do is rename the team but not the system to the DevOps development and operation team. Instead, they rename the two teams as the Agile and DevOps team respectively. In this case, the developers usually strive to deliver changes rapidly, and operations continue to deliver slow deployment, which inclines to be in terms of quality, which may not be acknowledged in terms of urgency in the system development. Moreover, the automation done by these teams does not serve the right purpose thus making it inefficient at the end of everything else or after the activities of the assigned teams.

One should understand that without bridging the "Dev" and "Ops," one cannot create collaboration, which is as a result of more repeatable or high code delivery quality of the application for consumption. In case one has not developed the team into a considerable DevOps team and operation together, chances are high that there will be no continuous integration, delivery and quality of the whole process to succeed.

In some instances, signs of dysfunctional can be detected when people are not using the Agile team, though there are many scenarios that suggest one can use Agile without DevOps but not DevOps without Agile. Therefore, what it depicts is that one cannot develop a high-quality application without involving DevOps in the system. There is continuous implementation of the software in most organizations, but some do not embrace its existence, making it more difficult to adopt by the organization. If, by any case, one is trying to adopt the delivery of a waterfall project, one must be sure to release the product once or twice a year to make it relevant and adaptable in the system. The code may not change every day, but there is a need for modification which may arise now and then. All these depend on the client's feedback on what they want, expect and how their products should look like to make it effective. In case one is not willing to actualize the whole process, they should be ready to fail. Deployment to production can also be done in such a way that the automation process is free of any defect which may arise.

When one finds themself in such a situation, it is high time to find an agile coach or those who can help in transforming. The investment in DevOps should pay off at the end of the day, and if in case it does not pay back the investors, it means that there is something wrong in the process or during implementation.

Normally, failure is not an option in the DevOps adoption in the organization. Nevertheless, the cultural aspect of the organization tends to play a major role in DevOps adoption. These cultural aspects may deem to be the difficult part of DevOps adoption. However, DevOps may have all that it takes to make everything right, but the mindset of the personnel in the organization determines the result and whether it leads to failure or success. There are some of the organizations which are risk-averse and are not ready to take any risk by adopting DevOps in their system. The mindset of the leaders in these organizations is hard to change since they will always prefer the old system they have been using from the past. Some are afraid due to public shaming, closed doors, or scolding by management, which may exist during deployment to production. One should understand that culture is not always conducive for the DevOps since DevOps comes with its own culture, one that has to be followed to the letter. As such, many organizations are afraid of adopting DevOps due to the fear that a stringent culture may not be easily adopted by developers. For that reason, many tend to shy away from the developing and operation processes of DevOps, which are demanding and have high resource requirements.

Furthermore, failures should be treated as special and as a learning opportunity for the developers. Some organizations take it a step further, and they never give room for conceptualizing the whole process or make an attempt to understand what has happened or the reason for failure. Such organizations are hard to deal with since they tend to make life difficult for their employees and even for themselves to adapt to new technology advancement. For one to reverse such situations, they need to get the best out of everything within the shortest time possible. Importantly, failures should be shared and made clear for clarification.Anyone who needs help must acknowledge such a need and give reasons for why they need assistance. It is only those who help themselves who can be helped, and in this case, when the failed organization is in a position to acknowledge, accept, and seek help, that is when the company can be helped. In most cases, organizations fail to seek help from the experts thinking that the organization is perfect and does not deserve to be helped. That mental schema is very wrong and should be avoided by all means.

Steps to DevOps Success

Since its inception, people have been debating the success of DevOps, or lack of, in the IT circles to determine its long-term fate. Some consider it as revolutionizing IT operations, while others regard it as a marketing fad. There has been a rapid growth prediction on this concept, which people have been capitalizing on over the years. In fact, there has been an improvement for the last decade regarding the same concept which make things to work on different perspectives of the business dealings. Here, DevOps failure has been largely blamed on people who do not understand how it operates or how it works—people who do not understand the different aspects of the software which make it legible. These people cannot realize the value of the software, and to some extent, cannot understand anything concerning IT development in the world today.

Therefore, people should prepare for the cultural shift that came with the DevOps adoption where people must integrate tools needed for transformation for a single entity. These cultural shifts mark the beginning of DevOps' success in an organization where the teams can master the code system of DevOps and how they develop. Though it is a difficult challenge to face such shift in cultural practices, care should be taken not to arbitrate the set goals and objectives of achieving full DevOps adoption.

Most DevOps adoption success stories begin with the top management team, who accepts the idea, then passes it to junior staff who are ordained to be part of the implementation team. There is a need to disassociate name or rank with the function one has to take in the process of developing, implementing, and delivering the DevOps code to responsible company needs. The value of each team member should be brought on board to make it viable and achievable project.

In case one needs to shift the cultural value of the company, there is a need to shift the incentives as well to make such change effective and welcomed. Moreover, some organizations prefer to work on-call where there is a high probability that one can understand the prevailing challenges in the process. From this experience, organizations can identify different potentials and capabilities among the developers and operators team where they can assign different tasks according to the speculation. By doing so, the organization can facilitate faster production thus increases the turnover.

Ultimately, the organization must encourage creation of continuous integration and delivery platforms. Here, the developers ought to get full information about what they need to do. For example, they should receive accurate and up-to-date data needed for the production. Such information eases the deployment process, and the developer can easily build on the appropriate approach to develop, run, and monitor code in the system. Moreover, there are major bugs that must be handled and presented accurately to developers to help them diagnose the software used in the organization. From this point, the DevOps team is to take care of the service lifecycle thus making an effort worth the investment put into it by creating good planning, deployment, and maintenance of the software.

Chapter Six:
Signs of Dysfunctional Processes in DevOps

The DevOps team is understood to be very vital in an organization's setup because it has the responsibility of ensuring that all operations run effectively. With the aid of continuous software deliveries and proper regulation of software products in technologically advanced firms, the system is made to be part of the operation, and to some extent, one does not need to adopt other non-functional applications that would otherwise be needed for supervision or oversight. Moreover, work is often made easier when the team members work together by sharing specific software skills and knowledge within the organization. Such practices are found to be quite useful when it comes to running an organization's base and effectively managing a company's software deliveries.

However, there are a few things that make the team incapable of performing its expected role to the extent that it causes work incompetency. It can also affect the whole system in such a way that it impacts the low level of software deliveries and poor management of the tech firm's database. From this perspective, it is prudent to discuss these signs of dysfunctional processes in DevOps that are responsible for diminishing the quality of software release in an organization. These facts and discussions are not limited or inclusive of all the factors which may influence the functionality of the DevOps system, but it gives more hints on what to expect and all those things which need to be avoided in the process. The expanse of all these factors depends on the size, nature, and business culture of the organization.

In most cases, self-centeredness in some specific individuals in the DevOps team will lower the work morale and performance of the organization. Clearly, optimism is encouraged in an agile team when members collaborate and assist each other. Such can be made possible and essential in the organization, but this optimism may be crushed and reduced due to the existence of one or two selfish members within the team who tend to lower the morale through discouragement or the exertion of a bad attitude on others. Such people are in any business setting, and most of them are inclined to be toxic and deprive others of progress. These people may present themselves as team members not open enough to share technical software skills and knowledge with other team members?

Furthermore, they may go as far as to hoard their code. If this is the case, it is a serious indication of a dysfunctional process in the team that members should seriously scrutinize. If the situation is serious enough, some even deserve to be disqualified or removed from the production team. In case this individual and their behavior is not addressed early enough, this character will lead to poor coordination and ineffective cooperation among team members. Treating such disease within the organization normally proves to be difficult, since most of these people are insiders used by the top managers within the organization to report any mischief. They are regarded to be the most useful people within the organization, even though they are useless to team members when it comes to DevOps development and operation.

Pair programming adopted from the Extreme Programming (XP) catalog of practices are regarded highly by the developers. It has been popularized to improve code quality and widen understanding of the product being developed through hands-on learning. However, some fallbacks exist during its delivery and development which are normal to any system developers. As usual, every business has to incur some losses before gaining the expected profit, or sometimes the profits exceed the expectation of the developers. As it has been depicted to be a process where two or more developers focus and work on the same code side by side to facilitate effective teamwork. The developed relationship reduces and eliminates narcissistic characters that exist in the organization's setup which proves to be toxic to progress. As a result, it ensures that team members freely share what they know and have without much contradiction during development and production of code. One should note that, when it comes to software development, teamwork matters most, and it ensures that all the processes are intact.

Furthermore, an effective DevOps team results in a group of peers whose definite objective is to ensure that the organization reaches its target. Also, it ensures that the organization achieves its goal no matter the risk that needs to be taken and other factors involved in the process. In some cases, there may be a seasoned or highly skilled member in the DevOps team who may feel that they are not suited for certain roles in the team, perhaps as the result of the insinuation that one considers themself more important than other members of the team. Most likely, it will result in refusal to perform certain important duties, unlike other members who freely engage themselves with the team tasks assigned to them. If these characters are encouraged, it may interfere with the overall success of the company, and this will be a clear sign of a dysfunctional process in the DevOps team. Therefore, there is a need for these individuals to be separated from team members and be positioned as either a coach or a technical trainer with the aid of leveling the position of the team in an organization. By doing so, the other team members can be creative and innovative in their projects without much hindrance from outside thus encouraging productivity and profitability of the firm. The product development is made easier and effective in the process which ensures that all the process goes smoothly.

Some DevOps teams may develop unpleasing habits which may deprive the organization productivity at the end of the financial year. These can be due to some factors which may be as a result of team members not following any process or rigor of any kind because they are practicing "Agile." It is always relevant for the DevOps to use the right process during service deliveries to ensure customer's satisfaction. So when DevOps team feels that they can customize just any process at any given time they wish, then it will lead to dysfunctional process in the team. So, the best solution to this problem is to direct that energy towards retrospection, where the team can explore opportunities for change. By doing so, they can change their current mindset that is causing this problem within the organization. Moreover, an effective reinforcement should also be ensured to allow gradual improvement of the team's mindset and also to train them to do so within the context of a designed approach within the retrospective system.

Additionally, miscommunication is conceived to be a clear sign of dysfunctional release process in DevOps, and it can cause unplanned outages in an organization. When there is little or no prediction in the release process for effective anticipation and contact problems in production due to miscommunication it tends to lead to many problems within the system. Also, the ineffective cost analysis and risks related to even the simplest of releases can inconvenience the production in the long run. In addition, when there is poor communication among members of the DevOps team, so many inaccuracies will be witnessed due to the mismanagement of information, and this will impact the organization to experience communication breakdown.

Furthermore, poor management of the environment in a release process will oblige the DevOps teams in charge of experimentation and qualification responsible for the release process to scramble over limited resources due to adversity. This will emerge as a result of the teams' inability to accurately anticipate environment contention issues. In this case, one will experience inconvenienced and frustrated when the whole project has to come to a halt and wait for a testing environment to be restructured at the last minute. No one likes such situations, and when it presents itself in the development stage, the responsible team usually feels discouraged and sometimes they may quit. To rejuvenate the process, there are some actions that need to be taken by the developers. Owing to the fact that restructuring will definitely result in unnecessary delays leading to time wastage and release of software products of poor quality.

Generally, it may be quite difficult to achieve continuous improvement of the team's mindset when they are surrounded by negativity that may impact the organization. Agile teams will require some time to develop an improved mindset, as it may take weeks or even months for the team to adopt the right state of mind. The DevOps team leader is responsible for developing an effective and positive mindset that fosters teamwork, genuine trust, and mutual understanding among team members. This will, in turn, improve the in-depth level of innovation and creativity among the team members, thereby boosting organization's productivity and ensuring that clients access quality services in terms of software deliveries. Most firms have currently resorted to employing high-performing technicians who are accorded the role of training, coaching, and mentoring the DevOps team members. By doing so, they enable them come up with effective strategies for managing software deliveries and creating a job momentum that will favor both software developers and IT managers.

Similarly, a high level of communication should be enhanced by creating relevant meetings between data scientists and technology employers. Such discussions are very important considering matters at hand, and it also allows for high tech employees to give out their opinions and address their grievances to their employers in time. Conclusively, effective teamwork within the DevOps system will be enhanced if members practice equity within the organizational set up by willingly sharing their technical skills and knowledge. Such actions are very important and should be taken seriously where development of DevOps is concerned.

In every IT firm, DevOps assume a major role in ensuring that there are effective software management and efficient deliveries. In most cases, these processes may be rendered ineffective due to some unfortunate eventualities that may arise from either IT managers or the DevOps team or even from the environment.

Sometimes an IT company may be located in an insecure area where IT employees feel unprotected from physical harm that may arise from bandits who surround that location. For instance, the company may have been situated in slums, where the crime rate is quite high due to unemployment and the existence of deadly gangs that are ready to steal and kill to earn a living. One or two members of the DevOps team may be attacked on their way home from work, impacting physical damage, serious health problems, or even death. This may interfere with DevOps' entire process due to loss of a member. Without any doubt, insecurity is a pure sign of dysfunctional process in DevOps team. By any means, such behaviors should be monitored to ensure that the system operation runs smoothly. However, it is the duty of the development and operation team to ensure that all the functionality is within reach of everyone involved.

A group of software developers may have worked in an IT company for a longer period and for that matter, expect to be promoted to a higher position because of their competency and job commitment. However, the firm may fail to recognize their deeds and ignore their call for promotion, making the DevOps team develop a negative attitude towards the company. Discouraged, these system developers may lower their concentration on work, thereby slowing the process of software deliveries and reducing the company's products. This will cause a dysfunctional process in the release of software products that may narrow the company's profit margin.

Motivation is important in any organization because it will often boost employees' morale to perform much better when carrying out their duties. Motivation can be done in several ways, and it can be either in terms of financial benefit, which includes salary increments, or even through mentorship programs. In any IT firm, software developers need much support from the organization's management team because of their responsibility in managing the company's database, a crucial role to the department and organization. Without motivation in an IT firm, the company is likely to experience lower level of attention by the system developers to perform their respective roles.

Increased level of corruption within the IT staff is also a sign of a dysfunctional process in the DevOps team because it will promote favoritism, which will create a toxic working environment, thereby building tension among members of the DevOps team. Considering other workers to be much more special than others will only create enmity within the organization, thereby lowering the level of coordination and cooperation among the team members. IT managers and directors should therefore ensure that they promote equity in dealing with members of the DevOps team to make every member feel a sense of value and appreciation. Failure in these companies to carefully highlight their objectives and policies to the DevOps team may also create irrelevancy when it comes to data management. When a firm is employing a DevOps team, members of this team should be obliged to stick to the company's policies and objectives to enhance sufficient delivery of software products.

Increased level of expenditure by the DevOps team may lead to financial shortages, thereby making the company not achieve its financial goals. The DevOps team may have been allocated with a substantial amount of funds by the finance department to enable them to run their operations smoothly and conveniently, but due to poor management of funds by the DevOps team, financial breakdowns might be witnessed leading to lowered software production and slowed release into the market economy. The IT Company will, in turn, incur financial losses leading to reduced profits in the IT Company. Poor management of funds is, therefore, a sign of the dysfunctional process of the DevOps team.

Recruitment of unskilled and incompetent technicians in the organization can lead to failure in the DevOps system due to ineffective processes. If the DevOps team consists of members who lack efficient technical skills and knowledge, the organization's goals will not be achieved to the latter. For any IT company to rise to the top, it will require quality service in software deliveries, and this will only be granted by a highly qualified DevOps team that consists of members who are technologically oriented, highly-skilled, and knowledgeable on software production. So before the DevOps team is selected, the department in charge of recruiting workers should thoroughly scrutinize the DevOps team and ensure that they have the right technological skills to facilitate quality smooth running of operations.

Limited ability to deliver multiple simultaneous releases in the organization affects service delivery. There may be many releases to be done in the IT company, but due to inefficient human resources and the inability of software developers to create continuous software delivery, there will be lower production of the company's software products.

Laziness portrayed by the DevOps team may also be one of the causes of a company's downfall. If the team members are not committed to their roles as expected, it may lead to a slow process of service delivery, thereby reducing the company's productivity. Failure of the DevOps team their work sufficient time will make an IT company experience losses that are least expected.

Failure of the DevOps team to conduct effective market research on their products may lead to poor sales of the software products. An effective team should take a reasonable amount of time to identify potential consumers and maintain them so that there may be the consistency of sales on the software products, thereby enabling the financial stability of the DevOps team. Poor market research should therefore be considered as a sign of dysfunctional process.

Poor planning and inefficient management of the software's database by the DevOps team may increase the level of incompetence in the IT firm. It may also interfere with the company's confidentiality on matters considered to be of high regard due to mismanagement of information by the DevOps team. This may, in turn, result in misunderstanding between the IT managers and software developers in an organization.

Chapter Seven:
The Future of DevOps

When discussing DevOps future and the road map that the technology is following, industry savants tend to concentrate on the bleeding edge, which comprises new technologies, management styles, and deployment techniques that seem to arise from nowhere. It is not predictable to determine where people are heading to in managing DevOps. Moreover, it is evident that the future of technology advancement is right before our eyes, and we cannot run from it. The only thing left right now is to embrace the new technology more so the DevOps application. Besides, the world of infrastructure as code is rapidly being congested by serverless networks, which already exists in the software workspace that is full of container technologies.

In a fast, high-tech developing world, software developers and technical leaders are trying to identify signs that an idea is creating a level of equilibrium and willing to get a head start that can allow them to strategize themselves. On that note, technology firms tend to take advantage of the uptrend and coming technical landscape, which has dominated the market lately. It is quite evident that there are widespread collaboration and effective communication between software developers and IT professionals due to DevOps culture narrowing the world into a global technological hub, which allows almost every individual to easily access information that they may require. These have created a need in the market gap, where every individual tends to cope up with the new technology. The DevOps manner of traveling is essentially a continuation from role to culture, and it will not be surprising to see rising and future generations adopting it as their daily way of living. The technology expected in the future can be predicted by looking at advancements dominating the world today, and people seem to engross themselves in the ever-changing and new marvels unveiled in the sector each day. This culture is now being adopted in almost every sector in the market economy, and governmental departments are not exempted. Everyone is now feeling the need to be technologically advanced because the world has changed greatly with time.

Evidently, there have been more worries for software developers in the world today. However, it should not be a problem for many as we continue to discover the power of new technology. Soon, tech firms will not have to be so much worried about security issues as the DevOps team is going to possess a renewed focus on security backed by three essential elements, namely, development, operations, and application delivery. Security will be created into the entire DevOps system, which will reduce vulnerabilities. There will be an ultimate combination of DevOps culture and security practices that will enable DevOps software systems to automate and enforce security policies in the current and future technology-dependent society.

Increased agility and a more scalable system will have to be developed by DevOps teams shortly to allow for concepts and methodologies like continuous integration and continuous release to be explicitly implemented, whereby automation will assume an even larger role. Revenue from digital modification and transformation and related software products and services will increase to 127 percent by 2020 as foreseen by IDC. This will occur due to rapid and consistent purchasing of software deliveries and products in the market economy which will become important and basic requirements in tech firms.

Operations will still have to be one of the fundamental requirements in the tech firms in an advanced evolving way, and essential data models will have to be created by data scientists. Data scientists will have to focus on building more developed software to enhance effective storage and delivery of quality information in a highly computerized world. This will leave operations engineers with the responsibility of deciding the best infrastructure approach to be used for each software solution, be it a containerized application or a serverless one. Sufficient computer processing power will have to be one of the major concerns of software operations engineers to enhance reliable processing of huge amounts of data being streamed and trained for machine learning. So it is quite evident that code awareness is going to be improved by these engineers to enable software developers better understand and evaluate the infrastructure requirements of applications and data pipelines. Furthermore, for this to be made possible, there will need to be mature coordination between software developers and operations team, as they are the ones responsible for creating the basic roots of computer progression.

Using DevOps teams will lead to a vast increase in data-driven applications, which in turn will promote technological invention and innovation in current business enterprises. The influence of such products on the market will support the rise of a more technically advanced economy, which will change the way goods and services are being purchased. As business is the driving factor behind the success of any economy, governments have already begun handing out subsidies to support technological growth and development in their respective countries to create more technologically-minded individuals. So the government is supporting the DevOps team and working hand in hand with the team as they need their technical brilliance to spread in all government sectors to improve the country's economy. So the DevOps team is going to experience even extensive government support soon.

DevOps are continually growing and developing their software skills in the industry. Moreover, development and operations teams are spreading their wings into a more developed and reliable, high-performance delivery world and this is going to make the DevOps culture be adopted by numerous companies that are interested in benefiting from their technological skills and knowledge to enhance them develop their software competency. So in the near future, we shall witness the DevOps culture being practiced in almost all tech firms, institutional facilities, and even in the health sector to enhance efficiency in service delivery.

The extensive use of infrastructure as code will ensure more flexibility when determining the server location by changing the code description. These can be done as soon as the application is installed in the organization system to ensure that there are efficiency and effectiveness in operation. However the people are expected to write codes so that they all can interrogate the large bodies of log reports to enable them to predict what next is required. By doing so, they can create efficiency of the system where future changes can be demonstrated early enough to evade any challenges which may inhibit the firm from functioning well. Besides, the code produced using automated services, which are well implemented by the DevOps team ensure flexibility in the system. One would not prefer to have a system that is vulnerable to changes and cannot adapt to new demands. For this reason, developers will thrive on producing the best codes for the organization which will withstand all situations. Stable code will be easily advanced by the experts whenever the need arises.

Software developers will be obliged to adopt the DevOps philosophy in their work procedures. This is due to the increasing number of Artificial Intelligence-driven apps and algorithms that have become rampant in the high tech world. To counteract the incoming competition, they have to keep pace and change with changes which may arise in the tech world. Moreover, DevOps strategies and methodologies will be expected to be their universal option in dealing with automated pipelines, maintaining, and testing numerous integrated models in the software production chain. That has to be integrated into the system by the DevOps development and operation team to ensure that all other inputs and outputs match the organization's goals and objectives. In turn, it will augment higher production of software products, thereby increasing their level of sales. By doing so, the sales margin will increase, making the organization prosper and generate high profit margin.

Final Words

A great foundation of work will be built on the DevOps team when there is trust and respect, which may take time to develop. The main responsibility of the leader of the agile activity team will be to improve the mindsets of the team members and to build mutual trust. One ought to understand the current trend and develop a friendly environment within the workstation to enable software developers to work in an encouraging atmosphere. Doing so will enhance efficiency. However, the team leader is indebted to promote effective collaboration between the team members to foster innovation and creativity in the IT firms so that DevOps team members will work closely enough to learn from each other. Important technological skills and knowledge need to be freely shared among the team members to improve work competency and to come up with quality software products' and to speed up software deliveries. Therefore, IT managers need to tentatively consider the technological skills and expertise when recruiting the DevOps team members to avoid poor service delivery, low quality of software products and to ensure that consumers are served to their expectations.

Furthermore, an IT company should ensure that it is well equipped with quality technological tools to ensure effective facilitation of work done by the

DevOps team. Technological equipment such as the latest model of computers and mobile phones should be granted to members of the DevOps team. These are to increase their concentration and to enable them to efficiently deliver their services in a more relevant way. Moreover, it eliminates errors unlike traditional and outdated software products and tools where the result proves to be faulty. IT managers should ensure that they provide close supervision on the team's work to ensure that correction is carefully made where there is a mistake. By doing so, they help the DevOps team members come up with better strategies to handle the technical problems in the system with a proper sense of responsibility and understanding. Critically, the DevOps team should work strictly per the company's policies and objectives to reduce irrelevancy in the organization. When this is considered, the IT Company will be able to carefully create a channel towards its goals achievement and the organization's targets will be easily reached.

When a DevOps team is performing highly, the organization should recognize their efforts by motivating them through salary increments, promotion of the team members, and mentorship programs. Such incentives boost the team's morale and working spirit, thus promoting high productivity. Besides, increased level of profit will be realized when this is carefully considered by the DevOps team. The company will experience a high profit margin due to the careful attention the DevOps team has on their work. Effective management of software products should be ensured by the DevOps team to avoid unnecessary software breakdown that may arise due to ignorance and carelessness of the DevOps team. Therefore, the DevOps team should learn to appreciate the technological tools and equipment they have at their disposal and use them relevantly in the organization to create work competency and to achieve the organization's goals and objectives.

Per-Olof Ågren

69 teknikfilosofiska fragment

Aforismer i informationsåldern